VERTICAL VEGETABLES

VEGETABLES

SIMPLE
PROJECTS
that
DELIVER
MORE
YIELD
in
LESS
SPACE

AMY ANDRYCHOWICZ

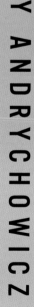

COOL
SPRINGS
PRESS

Inspiring | Educating | Creating | Entertaining

Brimming with creative inspiration, how-to projects, and useful information to enrich your everyday life, Quarto Knows is a favorite destination for those pursuing their interests and passions. Visit our site and dig deeper with our books into your area of interest: Quarto Creates, Quarto Cooks, Quarto Homes, Quarto Lives, Quarto Drives, Quarto Explores, Quarto Gifts, or Quarto Kids.

First published in 2018 by Cool Springs Press, an imprint of The Quarto Group, 401 Second Avenue North, Suite 310, Minneapolis, MN 55401 USA. T (612) 344-8100 F (612) 344-8692 www.QuartoKnows.com

Cool Springs Press titles are also available at discount for retail, wholesale, promotional, and bulk purchase. For details, contact the Special Sales Manager by email at specialsales@quarto.com or by mail at The Quarto Group, Attn: Special Sales Manager, 401 Second Avenue North, Suite 310, Minneapolis, MN 55401 USA.

10 9 8 7 6 5 4 3 2 1

ISBN: 978-0-7603-5784-2

Library of Congress Cataloging-in-Publication Data
Names: Andrychowicz, Amy, 1973- author.
Title: Vertical vegetables : simple projects that deliver more yield in less
    space / Amy Andrychowicz.
Description: Minneapolis, MN : Cool Springs Press, 2018. | Includes index.
Identifiers: LCCN 2018014378 | ISBN 9780760357842 (sc)
Subjects: LCSH: Vertical gardening.
Classification: LCC SB463.5 .A53 2018 | DDC 635--dc23
LC record available at https://lccn.loc.gov/2018014378

Acquiring Editor: Madeleine Vasaly
Project Manager: Alyssa Lochner
Art Director: Cindy Samargia Laun
Cover Design: Black Kat Design LLC
Page Design: Karen Minster
Layout: Tandem Books Inc
Photography: Tracy Walsh, except where otherwise noted
Project Builder: Chuck Pederson
Illustration: Christopher R. Mills

On the front cover: Photo by Tracy Walsh
On the back cover: Photo by Amy Andrychowicz

Printed in China

For my dad, for sharing your love of gardening and providing me with a constant supply of free plants, manual labor, guidance, and encouragement that fueled my growing passion for gardening. And for my mom, for sharing your love of plants and flowers and for showing me an appreciation for the beautiful things that inspire my creativity every single day.

CONTENTS

ACKNOWLEDGMENTS

Vertical Vegetables has been a fun and challenging project, and I am beyond thrilled to have completed such a monumental task! I'm the first to admit that this project was much more difficult than I ever imagined. I had to remind myself often to enjoy the ride, even during the times of chaos. Stressful and overwhelming at times, it has also been extremely rewarding and gratifying. Writing a book, especially when there are projects to build and plants to keep alive, is a colossal task, and one that I never could have done without my amazing support system of family, friends, and colleagues.

First and foremost, a huge thank you to my extremely talented brother-in-law Chuck Pederson, who designed and built several of the projects and also modeled for some of the photos in this book. I literally never could have done this without you! Your hard work and attention to detail were fantastic, and your ability to take my crude pencil sketches and turn them into beautiful vertical gardening structures was astonishing. This book was probably much more work than you expected it would be, and

I promise I'll never ask you to do it again (well, unless you want to).

A special thanks to my awesome and uber-supportive sister Lisa, who acted as the director and assistant and worked tirelessly behind the scenes to keep things running smoothly during the project builds and photo shoots. Thanks for your never-ending enthusiasm, and for your time and dedication to this project; you have no idea how much your help and support have meant to me throughout this process.

And to the rest of my amazing and incredibly supportive family, especially my mom, who rallied the troops at the 11th hour when I realized there was no way I was going to have everything ready in time for my first photo shoot. To my parents John and Nancy, my niece Breanna, and my nephews Cody and Justin for coming to my rescue and working so hard to get my gardens magazine-ready, and also for lending a helping hand whenever I needed you.

Thank you to my family for graciously allowing me to use their yards and gardens to build some of the projects, and for staging several of the photo shoots in the book . . .

although I have a sneaking suspicion you would have let me do that even if it wasn't for a book.

To my supportive husband Joel for his patience and understanding when our backyard and garage became staging grounds for my projects and were constantly cluttered with tools, plants, projects, dirt, and other supplies for most of the summer (although he would probably tell you they look that way every summer). For encouraging me to keep going when times got tough. For ordering food, providing snacks, buying wine, assisting me with the projects and photo shoots, understanding my absence on many evenings and weekends, and taking care of our house and cats while I was absorbed by the book. You are my rock, my light, my motivation to live life to its fullest, and I can't imagine ever having to face this crazy world without you.

To Tracy Walsh, the uber-talented photographer who shot all of the projects in this book. You are one of the most patient people I have ever worked with, and you have an incredible knack as a photographer. Every time I felt like I was falling apart, you always knew how to talk me off the ledge. You were the yin to my yang, a calming force to my anxiety, and the reasoning voice when I became flustered—and

darn it, you sure know how to make someone look good on camera! You're a true pro, and I can't imagine working with anyone else.

To my friend Al King, who showed the utmost patience when I learned the hard way that 16-foot-long pieces of cattle panel fencing do not fit into the back of a pickup truck, then went out of his way to get a trailer and drive the 20-mile round trip to pick up the panels at the farm supply store and deliver them to my house.

To my devoted readers, followers, and fans on GetBusyGardening.com—you have inspired, motivated, and encouraged me to continue over the years, even during the toughest of times, and for that I thank you! Without you, this dream never would have become a reality. I truly hope that you will love this book I've written for you.

To my Savvy Gardening sisters, Jessica Walliser, Tara Nolan, and Niki Jabbour, for your encouragement (peer pressure?) to write this book, and for your support, guidance, and friendship over the years. I'm thrilled and honored to join the ranks of authors with the rest of you brilliant ladies.

And finally, to the hard-working crew at Cool Springs Press—thanks for taking a chance on a new author and trusting me to get it done.

Structures for vertical gardening can be freestanding and portable, or they may rely on other elements of your yard for support. This rain gutter garden is freestanding. It adds growing capacity and also visual delight. See pages 179 to 184.

INTRODUCTION:
WHY GROW VERTICALLY?

A vegetable garden doesn't have to be purely functional—it can be beautiful too! Vertical gardening is all the rage right now, and it's one of the best ways to add unique character and charm to your vegetable garden. Though it's certainly not a new invention, vertical gardening has been given more attention lately because of all the fun and exciting spins on this old concept.

When they hear the term "vertical vegetable gardening," most people probably think of growing vining crops on trellises or other tall plant supports. But these days, it means so much more than that. Once you discover all of the innovative and extraordinary vertical gardening techniques that you can use to grow food, it will open your eyes to a whole new way of gardening.

Vertical gardening allows you to grow more food with less space and make use of areas where you otherwise wouldn't be able to grow anything, such as walls and fences, decks, patios, driveways, balconies, or porches. This is ideal for people with limited or no gardening space, and can provide exponentially more room to grow.

But vertical gardening isn't just for people with limited space. It's also fantastic for any gardener who may have a large garden plot but still wants to grow more food in the same amount of space or perhaps try something different. Or maybe they simply want to add beauty to their vegetable garden.

No longer do we need to just pound a few ugly stakes or flimsy wire tomato cages into the ground to support our plants out of pure necessity. Vertical gardening supports have become focal design features, works of art, and amazing architectural elements in the landscape.

Now they are part of the design, and people are planning their vegetable gardens around vertical structures rather than simply plopping them in as needed to stake or trellis their plants. Plus, with modern vertical gardening techniques, we can break the rules and grow food in unconventional ways that have traditionally been reserved for growing ornamental plants.

Vertical planters are highly space-efficient, but they can get top-heavy, especially after a rainfall, so a sturdy base is a necessity.

FINDING YOUR WAY AROUND

This book is for any gardener who wants to learn more about growing food vertically, including the benefits and techniques, design tips and ideas, choosing vertical gardening structures, materials and plants, and caring for your garden. Chapters 1 and 2 will become your guide to growing vertically and give you all the information you need to plan both a stunning and productive vertical vegetable garden.

In addition to being a guide for growing food vertically, this book also features a number of DIY projects for creating fun and unique vertical gardening structures. Chapter 3 is dedicated to vertical supports that are perfect for growing climbing vegetables. Whether you're looking to construct an architectural element, add character and interest to your garden, hide an unsightly area, create a private place to relax, or simply build strong growing structures for your vining vegetables, you will find projects here that will be perfect for your garden space.

Chapters 4 and 5 are filled with projects and inspiration for fun and unusual ways to grow non-vining crops vertically in different types of containers. These will allow you to utilize areas you never thought of before so you can grow food anywhere. These chapters are meant to inspire you to let your imagination run wild and come up with new and exciting ways to grow your own food!

There's a wide variety of projects in this book that were designed specifically for people of various skill levels. So if you're not particularly handy, don't worry; there are several projects that can be made by anyone and don't require any special skills or tools. If you're looking for more of a challenge, there are projects here for you too! Any weekend warrior will find plenty of satisfying projects and tons of inspiration to keep them busy well beyond building the structures in this book.

The goal of this book is not only to teach you how to grow food vertically. I also really want to inspire your creativity and encourage you— gardeners of all levels—to let your personality shine through by adding your unique flare to your vegetable garden. If you only have one takeaway from this book, remember this: vegetable gardens don't have to be purely functional; they can be beautiful too!

If you've never tried growing food vertically before, you're in for a real treat! Vertical gardening will revolutionize the way you grow food—hands down. I am absolutely hooked on growing vertically, and I'm confident that after reading this book you will be hooked on it too.

Are you excited and ready to take your vegetable garden to new heights with vertical gardening? Well, then keep reading!

Designing and building your own plant supports presents a fine opportunity to be creative and channel your inner artist, as with this freestanding and moveable easel planter. See page 119.

How I Found My Passion for Vertical Vegetable Gardening

The first time I tried growing my own food, I was living in a duplex that had a small yard and a few empty garden beds, so I decided to try growing green beans. I haphazardly planted a bunch of seeds in the ground and forgot about them until they started growing.

As the plants grew taller and began flopping over, I realized I needed to provide some sort of trellis for them. Not knowing any better, and because I found some stashed in the garage, I used basic wire tomato cages to support my crop. Soon my tiny garden was completely overgrown with unruly vines reaching for an adequate support. That summer I learned the hard way that vining crops such as pole beans need the right kind of support to grow on!

Not long after that, I bought my first house and excavated a large chunk of sod to make space for a vegetable garden. Since that fateful summer with the monstrous green beans, I knew to provide ample support for my pole beans, but I was still pretty clueless about vertical gardening. After a few years of struggling to grow substantial crops because the squash and cucumbers would crowd out the other plants, I decided to try trellising these larger vines to see if I could utilize my small garden space better. It was a wildly successful experiment, and that ended up being one of the best growing seasons I've ever had.

Since then, I've been passionate about vertical vegetable gardening, and I'm always trying to figure out new and creative ways to grow my crops vertically. As an avid DIYer, I quickly discovered that I have a knack for designing and creating projects; mixing that with my passion for vertical gardening ended up being the perfect match. These days, my number one goal is to not only grow a super-productive garden, but also make my vegetable garden just as beautiful as my flower gardens.

BENEFITS OF VERTICAL GARDENING

Growing vegetables vertically is a wonderful way to grow food—it has many great benefits. When you grow food vertically, your vegetable garden will be healthier, your crops will be better, and you will have more time to enjoy the summer. After all, who wants to spend all their free time weeding, feeding, spraying, and watering the vegetable garden?

LARGER HARVESTS: Whether you choose to trellis vining crops or plant vegetables in a vertical container garden, growing food vertically will result in larger harvests. Vining crops produce larger yields than bush or patio varieties, while vertical container gardens provide much more growing space than a traditional garden plot.

MORE FOOD IN LESS SPACE: When vining crops are grown on vertical supports rather than allowed to sprawl on the ground, they take up less space. In addition, growing vegetables in vertical container gardens allows you to grow more food in a smaller area and utilize spaces where you couldn't otherwise grow anything.

FUNGUS AND DISEASE PREVENTION: Trellising vining crops slows down the spread of soil-borne fungus and disease, keeping the plants much healthier. It allows better air circulation around the plants so that the leaves dry out faster, which will also help prevent problems with fungus and disease. Plus, the vegetables won't be prone to rotting like they are when left sitting on the ground.

PROTECTION FROM PESTS: Getting those yummy vegetables up off the ground will keep them out of the reach of hungry ground-dwelling pests. Growing vining crops vertically also makes it easier to protect the individual plants, since you can encircle susceptible plants with chicken wire or garden fencing to protect them.

LEFT: Hanging containers on a fence like this is an excellent way to grow non-vining crops such as herbs in a small space and utilize areas where you otherwise couldn't grow anything.

OPPOSITE: It's much easier to harvest vegetables such as cucumbers when they are hanging down from an arch than it would be if you had to hunt for them along the ground.

EASIER TO HARVEST: Vertical structures that bring your crops up to eye level make them much easier to harvest, and growing vining crops vertically means you no longer need to bend down to hunt for your food on the ground. Plus, vegetables will hang down from their growing support, making them easier to spot.

GORGEOUS VEGETABLES: Simply put, vegetables grown vertically are prettier than crops grown on the ground. The fruits grow straight when trellised, since gravity pulls them down. Plus, there won't be ugly yellow spots on vegetables such as cucumbers and squash, which happens when they are left lying on the ground.

CLEANER CROPS: Whether you grow food crops vertically in container gardens or by trellising the vines, vegetables that grow upward are cleaner than plants grown on the ground, since soil doesn't splash up on them.

ADDS BEAUTY AND PRIVACY: Growing food vertically adds beauty and visual interest to the garden, and vertical structures can be used in amazing ways to create privacy, hide unsightly areas, or add garden rooms and secret spaces to your yard.

EASIER MAINTENANCE: Vertical vegetable gardening makes laborious chores such as weeding, watering, fertilizing, and controlling diseases and pests much easier. Growing crops in vertical container gardens also makes maintenance easier, since problems like weeds, ground-dwelling pests, and soil-borne diseases will basically become nonexistent.

MORE SUN EXPOSURE: If you have a shady garden, vining crops can grow up and into the sun, where they will be able to thrive better than those left growing on the ground. Plus, when you grow food in vertical container gardens, you can place your garden wherever you have sun, such as on a wall, fence, or patio, or even on your driveway.

Gardens everywhere are filled with creative ways to train and support plants. Choosing the best type and configuration of the structures in your garden takes some planning and forethought. Using two arches over the center garden path creates a living tunnel in my small vegetable garden plot.

1

VERTICAL GARDENING BASICS

MY FAVORITE THING about vertical vegetable gardening is that I can use my creativity to grow food in fun and unique ways! There aren't any hard and fast rules for selecting the types of vertical gardening structures to use, which means our options are basically unlimited.

However, there are a few things to keep in mind when choosing vertical gardening supports to ensure that your crops will grow their best and be easy to harvest and maintain. You want to be sure that the structures will mesh perfectly with the size of your crops and become gorgeous additions to your garden rather than unintended eyesores.

To avoid any epic vertical gardening faux pas, it's a good idea to come up with a plan for your vegetable garden before you start building vertical gardening structures. So I encourage you to first sit down to plan out your vegetable garden, making a list of all the crops you want to grow. Then start brainstorming ideas for how and where you will incorporate vertical gardening structures based on your plan.

As you design your vertical vegetable garden, you may also want to think about the types of materials that you will use and any budget constraints you may have. When it comes to building your own vertical gardening structures and supports, it's important to use materials that will not only fit with the size and height of the plant, but will also work for your budget. Items that are readily available tend to cost less than materials that are difficult to find, and this is one of the main deciding factors when it comes to choosing materials.

In this chapter, we discuss the basic vertical gardening techniques, the different types of vertical gardening structures, things to consider that will help you decide which structures will work in your garden space, how to choose the best supports for the crops you want to grow, and options for selecting materials to use for DIY structures.

Caging is a technique that is commonly used for growing tomatoes, but it could also be used to support other vegetable crops in the garden or in containers.

Staking is a simple way to give extra support to plants such as determina tomatoes so they won't flop over when they're heav with fruit.

VERTICAL GARDENING TECHNIQUES

Some of the vertical gardening techniques discussed throughout this book may be unfamiliar to new gardeners. Understanding these common terms will help you plan your vertical vegetable garden and choose the best type of structure for each of your crops.

TRELLISING: Trellising is a technique for growing vining or branching crops vertically. It's also is a general term that is used in reference to any type of vertical support, not just trellises.

STAKING: Staking is a common practice in vertical gardening and a popular way to trellis plants that don't send out tendrils or have twining stems. It can also be used simply to give extra support to non-vining crops so they won't flop over when they're heavy with fruit.

CAGING: Caging is a vertical gardening technique in which the plant is encircled in a cage. It can be used to grow any type of vining or branching plant, such as indeterminate tomatoes.

TRAINING: Many types of vining crops, especially those that don't grab on to the structure on their own, will need to be trained to grow vertically. Training simply means showing the plants where to grow and attaching them to the support if necessary.

VERTICAL CONTAINERS: Vertical container gardening is a broad term that is used to describe gardens that are grown in stacked planters, wall pockets, hanging baskets, or any other type of container that is off the ground.

Plant clips make it easy to train vines to grow vertically. Simply unclip the vine once it grabs the trellis on its own, and move the plant clips up the structure as the vines grow taller.

How Plants Climb

Some vegetables will naturally climb a vertical gardening support on their own, while others can easily be trained to grow vertically. To help choose the right type of structure, it's important to understand how plants climb.

Tendrils—Vining vegetables such as cucumbers, peas, and squash send out shoots from the main stem, called tendrils, that will wrap around anything they touch. These types of plants aren't always great climbers on their own and may need to be trained to grow vertically.

Twining stems—Pole beans and hops are examples of vining crops with twining stems that will wind around a vertical support rather than sending out tendrils. These types of plants are excellent climbers on their own and don't usually require much training.

Long branches—Though technically not climbers, plants with long, pliable branches—such as indeterminate tomatoes, raspberries, and blackberries—can be trained to grow vertically by using ties or plant clips to attach them to a support.

TOP: Many types of vining crops use tendrils to attach themselves to a structure. These types of plants aren't always great climbers on their own and will likely need to be trained to grow up a vertical gardening support.

FAR LEFT: Vining crops like pole beans and hops having twining stems that wrap themselves around a structure and are excellent climbers on their own.

LEFT: Cane fruits and indeterminate tomatoes won't climb a structure on their own, but they have long, pliable branches that can be trained to grow vertically by tying the branches to a vertical support.

VERTICAL GARDENING STRUCTURES

There are many types of structures you can use for growing food vertically, with virtually unlimited room for creativity. Take some time to think about which structures will work best for the vegetables that you plan to grow and will also fit into your garden space. Here's a sampling of different options for vertical gardening structures to help get you started.

TRELLISES: A trellis is probably the most well-known type of vertical gardening support, and trellises can come in many different shapes and sizes. But generally speaking, a trellis is a flat structure that can either be freestanding or attached to something else, such as a wall or fence.

ABOVE: An overhead arbor is often employed to create a gateway into a garden. This simple arch made from PVC and wire adds wonderful height over the top of the short gate. The thick vines also create a lovely privacy screen.

LEFT: Trellises can be freestanding or attached to something else, like this one that's built onto the back of a large planter box.

ARBORS: An arbor is a structure that is frequently found at the entrance of a garden or over the top of a pathway. It's common for arbors to have latticework on the sides that is perfect for vining crops to grab on to.

TEEPEES: Teepees are fun structures that are easy to make. They can be as simple as a few twigs collected from the yard tied together at the top with twine, or as solid as the project in this book that is made out of 8-foot sturdy garden stakes.

PERGOLAS: Larger than arbors, pergolas are permanent structures that are commonly used to shade a patio, deck, or garden area. Arbors and pergolas are similar structures, and often the only difference is their size.

ABOVE: Pergolas covered by vining crops such as these hardy grapes are fabulous for creating a private hideaway in your yard where you can relax after a busy day.

LEFT: A teepee is probably the simplest freestanding plant support you can make. Teepee structures are not only fun for growing vining crops like pole beans; they can also be used to create tunnels like this one or forts for children to play in like the project on page 77.

ARCHES: An arch in the garden can take the form of an arbor or a pergola, or it can be an architectural element on its own. Large arches are often used to create tunnels or shaded pathways, and small arches can be used in the vegetable garden to double your growing space by training heat-loving vines over the arch and planting cool-season crops underneath.

OBELISKS: Obelisks are pyramid-shaped structures that have four sides and are traditionally found in formal gardens. They can be made out of any type of material, including wood, metal, or plastic, or even fashioned out of rustic materials like twigs and grapevines.

CAGES: Cages are often circular or square, and they can range in complexity from flimsy wire tomato cages to heavy-duty wooden cages. They can be as simple as a circular piece of leftover garden fencing or chicken wire tied together at the ends.

ABOVE LEFT: Arches can be constructed anywhere, and when built to a larger scale, they can be fun visual elements that draw attention to hanging garden fruits such as gourds, cucumbers, and melons. My squash arch is not only the focal point in my vegetable garden; it's also functional and gorgeous. Growing squash vertically allows me to keep it under control so it won't take over my small garden plot.

ABOVE RIGHT: Store-bought wire tomato cages work great for supporting determinate tomatoes, but indeterminate tomatoes need stronger structures, such as heavy-duty wooden cages, to support them.

TOP: A garden obelisk has the geometric shape of famous architectural structures such as the Washington Monument. They have a formal appearance and can be a little trickier to build because of the angle-cutting, but they can make lovely focal points.

LEFT: Hanging gardens, like living vertical walls, have become a very popular way to grow food. Small non-vining crops such as these salad greens thrive in vertical gardening containers.

RIGHT: Towers are simply stacked planting containers. You can buy stacked container growing systems that are specifically made for growing non-vining crops, such as herbs and salad greens, vertically. Systems like this one make it easy to get started quickly.

BELOW: A-frames and lean-tos are perfect for growing crops like cucumbers, and they make harvesting easier. Tall A-frames like this one are not only great for growing vining crops; they also provide additional growing space for smaller crops such as lettuce or spinach under the frame.

TOWER GARDENS: A tower garden is simply a tall or stacked container garden. A tower garden can be a tall structure that is made out of wood, metal fencing, or plastic, or even just a few stacked pots or planters.

A-FRAMES AND LEAN-TOS: A-frames and lean-tos are simple structures that can easily be made out of wood, twine, or metal garden fencing. They are almost identical, but an A-frame is shaped like an inverted V, whereas a lean-to leans to one side.

HANGING GARDENS: Hanging gardens can be anything from a few basic hanging baskets suspended from hooks, to more complex creations, such as vertical wall pockets, living walls, and picture frames.

THINGS TO CONSIDER

When you start thinking about all the different types of structures you could use to grow food vertically, it's easy to get caught up in the excitement and forget to think practically. But it's important to choose the right type of structure for each of the crops you plan to grow, and for the size and style of your garden. Here are some considerations as you plan your vertical vegetable garden.

WHAT DO YOU WANT TO GROW?

Before you get too excited and hastily start building vertical walls, arbors, and trellises, take some time to think about what types of vegetables you plan to grow. While you might think an arbor would look incredible standing at the entrance of your vegetable garden, if you never grow large crops like cucumbers or squash to cover it, it may end up looking silly just sitting there empty. Likewise, a vertical living wall may not be very useful to you if you already have a large vegetable garden plot with plenty of space for growing all of your crops.

PLACEMENT

Most vegetables need to be grown in full sun, so it's important to think about where you plan to put your vertical container garden, as well as the placement of tall supports such as arbors and arches. A north-facing fence or wall will shade the vertical pockets or living picture frames hanging on it, and tall structures placed at the south end of a garden plot can end up shading the rest of the garden.

Some of the most effective vertical gardens use a combination of structures and strategies. A-frames are excellent vertical gardening structures that make harvesting easy and can also look beautiful. This DIY A-frame trellis was made using pieces of wood that are attached together with nails.

GARDEN STYLE

Another thing to consider is the style of your existing garden space or landscaping. Vertical gardening supports are not only functional; they are decorative elements in the garden as well. If your garden style is informal and casual, then stately structures like arbors or obelisks could be overbearing. On the flip side, a rustic teepee made out of twigs, or a handmade bamboo trellis, may look awkward in a formal garden setting.

PROPORTION

Regardless of which vertical gardening technique you choose to use, be sure that the size of the structure is proportionate to the plant you wish to grow. Growing long vines such as pole beans, pumpkins, or hops on a 4-foot obelisk or fan trellis, or planting

ABOVE: A small fan trellis like this one would be great for supporting small crops like peas or determinate tomatoes, but it will be overwhelmed once the cucumber vines using it here are full grown and heavy with fruit.

LEFT: It's important to consider the style of your existing gardens when planning your vertical gardening structures. Using a bunch of bamboo stakes like this might make it look unappealing to some, and could also make harvesting difficult.

full-sized tomato or pepper plants in a living picture frame or small vertical pockets will be overpowering (and could end up being disastrous). On the other hand, if you want to grow small vining crops such as peas or mini melons, then a large trellis or arch tunnel is going to be superfluous.

In addition to the proportion of the structure to the size of the crops you plan to grow, think about the scale of the structure in your garden. Plopping a tall pergola or arbor in the middle of a tiny garden will likely overwhelm the space, while hanging a tiny living picture frame in the middle of a huge empty wall would look equally disproportionate.

TEMPORARY OR PERMANENT?

When planning which type of vertical gardening structures you want to incorporate into your garden, think about how they fit into your long-term plans. Large structures such as arbors and pergolas will become permanent fixtures in the landscape, while fan trellises, small arches, and tomato cages can easily be moved around as needed after each gardening season.

HEIGHT

The maximum height a vine will grow is different depending on the type of crop. Vines can stay short, growing only a few feet tall like peas

Grapes and other large vining crops need a tall support like this pergola to ensure they have plenty of room to grow.

ABOVE: A small support may seem adequate when you plant those tiny seedlings in the spring, but once vegetable plants become mature and heavy with fruit, weak structures can quickly collapse under all that weight.

LEFT: Vertical gardening structures usually make harvesting easier, but sometimes compact structures such as teepees or obelisks can make harvesting more difficult because they cause the vines to grow in a tight cluster, making it hard to reach the middle.

and mini melons, or they can grow to the tops of trees like pumpkins and watermelons—or anywhere in between. Make sure to choose a support that's tall enough so the vine will have plenty of room to grow. A wire tomato cage or small fan trellis would be sufficient for growing short vining crops, but longer vines such as beans and cucumbers will need taller supports.

STRENGTH AND WEIGHT

Once large vines such as squash, grapes, melons, and cucumbers are full of produce, they will become very heavy. You don't want a vertical gardening structure to collapse under the weight of heavy vining crops, so be sure to choose a support that is sturdy enough to hold the weight of the mature vines.

Weight is also an important factor for hanging vertical gardens. The soil in containers such as vertical wall pockets, hanging planters, and living picture frames will become very heavy once it's wet. So consider the weight of the finished project, and ensure that the place you plan to hang it, especially on a wall or fence, is strong enough to support that weight.

EASE OF HARVESTING

Harvesting is usually easier in a vertical vegetable garden, but choosing the wrong type of support can actually make it more challenging. Some types of structures, such as narrow obelisks or small teepees, make harvesting difficult because these compact structures keep the vines in a tight cluster, which makes it harder to find and reach the fruit growing in the center of the support. Tall structures, such as pergolas and arbors, can also make it difficult to harvest your vegetables. Getting out a ladder once or twice to harvest crops like grapes or hops isn't a big deal, but lugging the ladder out to the garden on a daily basis to harvest beans, cucamelons, or cucumbers is not very practical for most gardeners.

CHOOSING MATERIALS

When it comes to building your own vertical gardening structures, choose materials that will work with the type of structure you plan to build as well as the plants you want to grow. There are lots of wonderful materials that are great to use for building vertical gardening structures, and each one has pros and cons. Many times the final decision comes down to the availability of certain materials in your area and the size of your budget.

WOOD: Wood is easy to work with, readily available, and highly versatile. Since wood rots, especially any parts that are buried in the ground, choose a naturally rot-resistant lumber, such as cedar. Pressure-treated wood is usually much cheaper to buy than naturally rot-resistant wood, and it may be more budget-friendly. New pressure-treated wood is considered safe for use in vegetable gardens. However, wood that was treated before the early 2000s may contain arsenate, a chemical that can leach into the soil. That being said, new wood is still treated with chemicals, so it's up to you to decide if you want to use it in your vegetable garden or if you'd rather stick to using natural, untreated woods.

METAL: Metal is a common material used for making trellises, obelisks, and arches, and its beauty and durability are hard to match. Some of the projects in this book are made out of various types of metal, and if you know how to weld, you can build even more elaborate vertical gardening structures. The downfall of metal is that it can rust or develop a patina over time. Some metals rust faster than others, but it's not always a bad thing when they develop a heavy patina. Another thing to consider with metal is that some types of metal are very heavy, which may not be practical for building a tall vertical gardening structure.

GARDEN FENCING AND CHICKEN WIRE: Metal garden fencing is a wonderful material to use for building vertical gardening structures. It's inexpensive and easy to work with, and I'm willing to bet that most gardeners have leftover rolls somewhere. When it comes to choosing the type of fencing for your project, be sure to take into consideration the thickness of the metal. Fencing made out of thin metal, such as chicken wire (also known as poultry netting), isn't strong enough to stand up on its own and will need extra support to keep it from collapsing under the weight of vining crops. Fencing made from thicker-gauged metal, such as cattle panel fencing, is much heavier and can be used to build strong vertical gardening

How Strong Is Your Garden Fencing?

Metal garden fencing is usually labeled by the thickness of the wire (called the "gauge") used to create it. It sounds backward, but the smaller the gauge number on the label, the thicker the wire, and the stronger the fencing will be. So heavy-duty cattle panel fencing like the material used to build the large arch tunnel in this book (see page 74), is made of 4-gauge wire, whereas standard chicken wire fencing ranges from 19- to 22-gauge.

Vertical gardening containers should always have drainage holes in the bottom to keep plants from drowning. If the container you choose doesn't have holes, simply drill some into the bottom using a large drill bit.

Natural Materials

When it comes to finding materials for building your garden structures, you may not have to look any further than your own backyard. Vertical gardening supports can easily be fashioned out of branches, twigs, grapevines, or even the stalks of tall plants such as sunflowers or corn. These natural materials are free, which is a huge bonus, and in the fall when it comes time to pull your plants, you can simply toss the whole thing into the compost bin, support and all. But these types of structures are temporary and not very strong, so be sure to choose crops that will work with the structures you plan to build.

Garden fencing is a wonderful material to use for making your own DIY vertical gardening supports, but large vegetables like cucumbers can get stuck in the fencing as they grow.

Bamboo is a popular material to use for building vertical gardening structures such as teepees. It's easy to work with, strong, durable, and naturally rot-resistant.

structures. The biggest downfall of using wire fencing for growing crops vertically is that large vegetables can get wedged in the fencing voids as they mature.

POTS AND CONTAINERS: It's fun to find unique ways to use pots and planters in vertical gardening, and there are tons of gorgeous options. Always consider the full weight of the planted container when making your choice. And if a container does not already have adequate drainage holes, make sure the material will allow you to add them easily.

BAMBOO: Another type of natural material, bamboo is strong and rot-resistant, and it can be used to make very sturdy supports that will last for several years. Bamboo is great for staking plants and making simple structures such as teepees and trellises. If you're lucky

enough to have a dependable supply of bamboo readily available to you, then you're in business. But for others, bamboo can be difficult to find and expensive to buy.

UPCYCLED MATERIALS: When it comes to using upcycled materials to build garden structures, the options are limited only by your imagination. Many items can be found for pennies at secondhand stores and yard sales, or if you're lucky, you can get them for free! You may even find hidden treasures in your garage or shed that you can repurpose into vertical gardening structures like the upcycled garden tool fan trellis project found later in this book. However, if you plan to use antiques or vintage items, be careful using anything that was painted before 1978, because the paint could contain lead.

One of the best things about vertical gardening is that, even in a small space, you can grow just about any crop that you can in a large garden plot. Most types of vining vegetables traditionally grown in large gardens are also available in smaller sizes that are specifically bred for growing in containers.

2

CHOOSING WHAT TO GROW *and* CARING FOR VERTICAL GARDENS

MANY PEOPLE THINK they need to have a huge garden plot to grow a healthy crop of vegetables. That's simply not true. The best part about vertical gardening is that, even in a small garden, you can grow just about any crop that you can grow in a large vegetable plot.

Growing vining crops vertically rather than allowing them to sprawl along the ground means that you can grow more food in less space. And when you start looking at the assortment of miniature varieties and patio plants available on the market, it really opens up the options for the types of crops that you can grow vertically.

No more are monsters such as tomatoes, berries, and citrus reserved for growing in a large garden plot. There are wonderful varieties of patio plants for just about any type of crop you want to grow, which is great news for those of us who like to get creative with our vertical gardening spaces!

Another wonderful benefit of vertical gardening is that it's much easier to maintain a healthy and productive vegetable garden. Growing crops vertically keeps your food out of reach of ground-dwelling pests, helps prevent the spread of fungus and disease, and even makes arduous tasks like weeding, watering, and fertilizing much more manageable.

This chapter focuses on the various types of plants that thrive in a vertical vegetable garden, including the benefits and challenges unique to each one, planting tips, and the recommended types of support or vertical containers. You'll also learn how to take care of your vertical vegetable garden so that you don't have to spend your entire summer weeding, watering, fertilizing, and fighting pests and disease.

VEGETABLES BEST SUITED FOR GROWING VERTICALLY

When it comes to choosing which vegetables are best suited for growing vertically, the obvious choices are vining crops such as pole beans, cucumbers, and peas. Vining crops are great for covering trellises, arbors, and arches.

But vertical gardening doesn't limit us to only growing a handful of vining crops. There are numerous non-climbers that can be grown vertically too. When you start adding in living walls, hanging gardens, and vertical planters, your options for what you can grow vertically are almost unlimited.

Before I start listing all the vegetables that you can grow vertically, it's important to understand the difference between vining and bush varieties.

Generally speaking, there are two basic types of vegetable plants that you can grow in your garden: bush varieties and vining varieties. The main difference between the two, which is a very important one to understand when choosing plants for vertical gardening, is that vining varieties will grow on a trellis, and bush varieties will not. You can't always tell the difference between the two when looking at a plant, especially a small seedling, so be sure to always check the label or seed packet before purchasing.

Don't worry; you won't have to make any sacrifices when it comes to vertical vegetable gardening, because these days pretty much any type of vining vegetable plant also comes in a compact bush version. Below I have broken the list of vegetables down into climbers and non-climbers (which includes bush varieties) to make it easy for you to find the best plants for your garden.

Many traditional vining crops also come in compact bush varieties, which won't climb a trellis. So if you want to grow vining crops vertically, be sure to check the plant label or seed packet before purchasing to ensure you're getting the right type of plant.

CLIMBERS

Vining crops don't need a support to grow and produce, but they tend to take over the garden if left to sprawl on the ground. Growing vining crops vertically allows you to grow more food in the same amount of space.

Trellising climbers such as beans and peas is a common practice. But did you know that you can do the same with heavier vining crops, such as cucumbers and squash? Even the giant vines of gourds, melons, and pumpkins can be grown vertically. Here are the different types of climbers that you can choose from when deciding what you want to grow in your vertical vegetable garden.

CANE FRUITS

Cane fruits, such as blackberries and raspberries, grow on long, thorn-covered stems called canes. Though they aren't vines, the long, pliable canes can be trained and tied to a vertical gardening support.

Both blackberries and raspberries are perennial plants and very aggressive growers. The plants send out runners underground that can pop up anywhere, so make sure you plant them in an area where you don't mind them taking over, or keep them contained to a large planter box or raised bed.

Most varieties of blackberries and raspberries won't bear fruit on new canes—only on second-year canes. Once the second-year canes are done fruiting, they should be pruned from the plant to encourage new growth and higher yields, help prevent issues with disease, and keep the plant tidy.

BENEFITS: Cane fruits are fairly low-maintenance perennial plants that can produce lots of berries every year. Once established, they work great as a privacy screen or a living fence.

CHALLENGES: Cane fruits are aggressive spreaders, and they can take over the garden if not properly managed. They are also vulnerable to several types of diseases, but these can usually be prevented with proper pruning. Japanese beetles favor the leaves and can be a major problem on cane fruits. Raspberry cane borers and hungry birds can also be a problem. Plants might need to be protected during the winter so rabbits won't eat the canes.

PLANTING TIPS: The best time to plant cane fruits is in early spring or fall when the weather is cool. Plant cane fruits in an area that has well-drained soil, gets full sun, and is protected from harsh winds.

SUPPORTS: A large trellis would work great for growing cane plants. The branches can also be trained to grow up a wall or on a fence.

Cane fruits such as these raspberries have long, pliable branches that can be trained to grow on a trellis, wall, or fence. Simply tie the canes to the support, or use plant clips to hold them in place.

Cucamelons are relatively new to most gardeners, but they are becoming very popular because they are fun to grow. Cucamelons are prolific producers, and their dense vines will quickly cover medium to large structures. The small fruits taste like a cross between a watermelon and a cucumber, with a sour twist.

CUCAMELONS

This fun plant was introduced into the gardening world a few years ago and quickly became a huge hit with gardeners everywhere. Cucamelons look like tiny watermelons, and they are extremely productive plants.

I've heard the flavor described differently by many, but to me cucamelons taste like a combination of a cucumber and a water-melon, just like the name suggests, but with a sour twist.

This easy-to-grow vine has beautiful, dense foliage that can quickly cover a trellis, obelisk, arbor, or other vertical gardening structure. The best part about cucamelons is that they are disease-resistant and have very few issues with pests, making them a perfect addition to any vertical garden plot.

BENEFITS: Cucamelons are lightweight, prolific, and fast-growing. Furry creatures such as deer or rabbits—and insect pests—aren't usually a problem. Cucamelons are also disease-resistant.

CHALLENGES: Cucamelons can be challenging to grow from seed, and the seeds aren't always easy to find for sale. They aren't great climbers, and the vines tend to clump together at the bottom of the structure. Cucamelon vines want to grow horizontally along the ground rather than vertically, so they will need to be trained to grow evenly up a vertical structure.

PLANTING TIPS: Wait until the soil has warmed after the last frost in the spring to plant cucamelon seedlings in a full-sun location.

SUPPORTS: Choose a medium to large structure for growing cucamelons. Since they are lightweight vines, cucamelons are perfect for growing on trellises, arches, teepees, and obelisks.

CUCUMBERS

Many people hesitate to grow cucumber vines vertically because they're worried the cucumbers will rip off the vines once they start to mature. It's a common misconception, but rest assured—cucumber vines are plenty strong enough to support the weight of their fruit.

Cucumbers actually grow better when the vines are grown vertically rather than left to sprawl along the ground. Since gravity is on their side, the cucumbers grow straighter. Plus, they won't develop ugly yellow spots, which is a common problem when cucumbers are grown lying on the ground.

Growing cucumbers vertically also makes harvesting easier. No more bending and hunting for the cucumbers that are hiding in all that thick foliage on the ground. Trellised cucumbers also get better air circulation, which means they have less trouble with foliage disease and fungus caused by soil and water splashing up onto the leaves when it rains.

BENEFITS: Cucumbers are easy to grow from seed and are prolific producers. Because of their prickly texture, furry pests such as rabbits and deer don't usually bother cucumbers.

CHALLENGES: Insect pests such as cucumber beetles can be problematic, and squirrels like to eat cucumbers and their flowers when you're not looking. Foliage disease and fungus issues can also be major problems. Cucumber vines don't always find their way up a trellis, so they will likely need to be trained to grow vertically.

PLANTING TIPS: Wait until the soil has warmed after the last frost in the spring, and then direct-sow the seeds in a full-sun location.

SUPPORTS: Cucumbers can be grown on a medium to large trellis, or on a small arch or obelisk. Keep in mind that the vines will become heavy once the cucumbers start to mature and hang down, so be sure to use a support that is strong enough to handle their weight.

Trellised cucumbers grow straighter and have fewer issues with fungus and disease than do vines left growing on the ground. Rest assured, the vines are strong enough to hold the dangling cucumbers and don't need any extra support.

Grapes are perennial vines that can live for decades (though not every climate is suitable for them), so it's important to choose a strong, permanent structure—such as a pergola or an arbor—to use for growing them.

GRAPES AND HARDY KIWI

Grapevines and hardy kiwi vines are perennial plants that have similar growth habits and care requirements. Both types of vining fruits have stems that can be trained to climb up a growing support, and they can grow to be very tall.

The hardiness of these perennial vines will depend on the variety you choose, so it's important to research which ones are best for your growing zone. It can take anywhere from two to four years for these hardy perennial vines to mature enough to bear fruit, and the plants must be pruned regularly to maintain their shape and maximize fruit production.

Grape and hardy kiwi vines need a strong support to grow on—one that is tall enough to allow for plenty of growth. The vines can be trained to grow out horizontally across the support (as you see in vineyards), or you can allow them to grow over the top of a tall structure, such as a pergola or arbor, so that the fruits will hang down from the ceiling as they mature. Just keep in mind that, since the vines are perennial and can live for a long time (some grapevines can live for over 100 years!), you'll need to grow them on a permanent structure that is built to last for many years.

BENEFITS: Old vines produce several pounds of fruit that can be used for canning, making wine, baking pies, or snacking. (Kids love eating sweet grapes and kiwi fruits fresh from the vine!) The perennial vines are outstanding to use as a privacy screen or create small "rooms" in your garden.

CHALLENGES: Hardy kiwi vines are easy to grow and don't normally have any issues with pests or diseases. Grapevines, on the other hand, can be a bit more challenging. Japanese beetles love grapevines, and they can cause unsightly damage to the leaves. The grapevine beetle can also become a problem in large numbers, but it's very uncommon. Birds and squirrels sometimes enjoy snacking on grapes too.

PLANTING TIPS: Install the growing structure before planting so that you don't damage the vines. Plant the vines in the spring in an area that receives full sun. Young vines may need to be tied to the support until they grow long enough to coil around it themselves.

SUPPORTS: Both types of perennial vines require a strong, permanent structure, such as an arbor or a pergola.

HOPS

Thanks to the boom of small breweries and the increased interest of hobbyists brewing their own beer at home, growing hops in the home garden has become more popular than ever.

If you want to try your hand at growing hops in your garden, make sure you do your research so you understand what you're getting into. Hops are very aggressive perennial plants that can quickly take over—and sometimes even escape—the garden. They are also fairly high-maintenance plants, requiring a lot of pruning and training each year to produce the best crops, and they need a lot of water.

Hops have burst onto the home gardening scene with the rise in popularity of homebrewing. They are easy-to-grow perennial vines with winding stems and will quickly cover a vertical gardening structure. But be careful; hops can become invasive if they're not managed properly.

Hops vines grow to be very tall, but they are lightweight, so they don't require a large structure to support them. The vines will die back in the winter, and new shoots will grow from the ground each spring. Every year the new growth will need to be trained to climb on the support, but once they grab on, they're excellent climbers.

If you plant hops rhizomes in early spring, you could get a small harvest the first year. But it takes two to three years for the plants to mature enough to start producing substantial harvests. Since they are so popular right now, it might be tough to get your hands on some, but if you ask around you may be able to find a friend who's willing to share a few rhizomes with you.

BENEFITS: Hops are easy-to-grow perennial plants that don't have many pest or disease issues. The vines grow fast and are great to use as a privacy screen or to cover a large garden arch or teepee. Plus, you can brew your own beer!

CHALLENGES: Deer and rabbits will sometimes munch on the tender new shoots as they pop out of the ground in the spring. But once the vines grow taller, pests are usually turned off by the bitter flavor. Hops are very aggressive spreaders and can become invasive if not properly managed.

PLANTING TIPS: Plant rhizomes in a full-sun location where they will receive ample water. Consider planting the rhizomes in a planter box or well-contained raised bed to make it easier to keep them under control.

SUPPORTS: Any medium to large vertical gardening structure will work great for growing hops, as long as it's tall enough. Some people grow hops on strong twine or wire trellises attached to the side of a building, but an arbor, large arch, or tall trellis would work equally well.

Determinate versus Indeterminate Tomatoes

You may hear the terms "determinate" and "indeterminate" in regard to tomatoes and wonder what they mean. Those are fancy words that are used to distinguish the difference between the height and size of the two types of tomato plants.

For me, it's easy to remember the difference between the two when I think of the meaning of the words. Determinate means they have a determined or maximum size limit, and indeterminate means there is no set limit; the size is undetermined, which makes me think of large, vining plants.

Determinate tomatoes, also known as bush tomatoes, are varieties that don't grow to be very tall. These smaller, more compact plants can be grown in the garden, but they are usually marketed as "patio" or "container" plants since they grow very well in small spaces or pots. Though they don't grow as tall as indeterminate varieties, determinate tomatoes usually need some kind of support, such as a cage or stakes, to keep them from toppling over once they are heavy with fruit. Determinate tomatoes, such as Roma, tend to produce most of their ripe fruit in a concentrated period of time, making them popular for sauce making and other uses that demand a lot of tomatoes at one time.

Indeterminate tomatoes grow to be very tall and have long, vining branches that can be trained to grow on a vertical support. These heavy branching plants won't stay upright on their own; they need to be trained on a trellis or grown in heavy-duty tomato cages. Indeterminate tomatoes can grow to be monsters and are best suited for growing in a large garden plot rather than a container.

Most "patio tomatoes" are very compact, determinate types that produce plenty of fruit in a small space.

INDETERMINATE TOMATOES

When choosing indeterminate tomatoes to grow vertically, look for varieties like 'Big Boy', 'Beefsteak', or 'Sweet 100' (a few of my personal favorites). Indeterminate tomatoes aren't always labeled as such, but in my experience, any tomato plant that's not labeled as a "patio" or "container" variety is indeterminate. A quick internet search on the name of the tomato you want to grow will tell you for sure.

Though they grow long, vining branches, indeterminate tomatoes won't climb a vertical structure on their own; they will need to be trained and tied on to their support. Gently press the branches against the vertical support, and secure them in place using twist ties, flexible plant ties, or plant clips. Just be sure to tie them very loosely so the ties don't cut into the branches as they grow thicker.

Indeterminate tomatoes are fun to grow on tall vertical gardening structures—such as a large trellis, obelisk, A-frame, or lean-to trellis—or could even be trained to grow over a small garden arch. The fruit will hang down from the plant as it ripens, which not only makes harvesting easier, but it looks pretty amazing too.

BENEFITS: Indeterminate tomatoes are heavy producers and will yield much more fruit than determinate varieties. These tomatoes mature and ripen throughout the growing season for a continual harvest, rather than ripening all at once.

CHALLENGES: Tomato plants are prone to several diseases, and blight is probably the most well-known tomato ailment. Tomato hornworms, stink bugs, tomato fruitworms, and squirrels can also cause problems. Cracked fruit and blossom-end rot are also very common problems with tomatoes, both of which can be prevented with consistent watering.

PLANTING TIPS: Plant tomatoes in a full-sun location in late spring once the soil has warmed and all chance of frost is gone. Remove the bottom leaves from the stem before

The difference between determinate and indeterminate tomatoes is their size. Indeterminate tomatoes like these can grow very tall and are perfect for training on a vertical structure such as an A-frame or arch.

planting, and bury tomato plants deeply so that they will develop strong root systems.

SUPPORTS: Indeterminate tomatoes need a strong support to keep them upright. A medium to large vertical support—such as an A-frame or lean-to trellis, a heavy-duty tomato cage, or a large trellis—would be perfect for growing indeterminate tomatoes.

MELONS

Melon plants come in lots of different varieties and sizes. Some are ideal for growing vertically, but the monsters, such as giant watermelons, are not practical for vertical gardening. Melons can be challenging for many gardeners to grow. Melon plants are heavy feeders and need rich, fertile soil to mature and produce fruit.

Many home gardeners also find melons challenging to grow because melon plants like it hot and need tons of sun, and most varieties require a long, warm growing season (at least 80 days) to produce mature fruit. So, for northern gardeners like myself, seeds will need to be started indoors to give them a head start.

Most types of melons can be grown vertically, but make sure you know how large they will get. Miniature melons are perfect for growing on small supports, but full-sized varieties will need to be grown on large, strong supports.

Melons aren't great climbers, and they usually need to be trained to grow up vertical gardening supports. Once the fruit starts to grow large, be sure to swaddle it with an old t-shirt or other piece of cloth to support the weight and avoid damage to the vine.

If you want to try growing melons in your garden for the first time, start with an early variety (less than 65 days) such as 'Minnesota Midget' cantaloupe. Just keep in mind that short-season mini melons will have smaller fruit than their full-season counterparts.

BENEFITS: Melon plants are easy to grow from seed and are fast-growing vines. Their dense foliage can fully cover a vertical gardening structure, adding a stunning visual element to the garden or creating a lovely screen. Furry pests, such as rabbits and deer, don't favor melon vines.

CHALLENGES: Melons are closely related to squash, and therefore are susceptible to the same ailments as squash plants (see page 46). Squash borers and squash bugs can be a major problem for melon plants, as can diseases, such as powdery mildew. Melons are finicky about their soil, and many varieties require a long growing season to mature and produce fruit.

PLANTING TIPS: Wait until the soil warms in early summer before direct-sowing the seeds, or start seeds indoors two to four weeks before you plan to transplant them into the garden. Take care not to disturb the roots when transplanting to avoid stunting the growth of the plant.

SUPPORTS: Mini melons can be grown on smaller supports—such as trellises, obelisks, or small arches—but full-sized melon vines will need a bigger and stronger support, such as a large arch, arbor, or pergola.

Supporting Heavy Vegetables and Fruit

Even though it doesn't look like it, most vines are strong enough to hold the weight of the vegetables or fruit hanging down from them. Don't worry; cucumbers and small varieties of melons, gourds, and squash will not rip from the vine as they mature.

However, bigger crops—such as pumpkins, larger varieties of gourds, and melons—may need to be supported if they are hanging down from the vine. To give them extra support, you can use an old t-shirt or other piece of fabric (some people even use pantyhose!) to make a sling to support each one as it matures.

Tie both ends of the sling to the trellis and secure it tightly so it can handle the extra weight. Don't tie your sling too tightly around the fruit; make sure to leave room for growth. You can loosen it up and retie it as your crops grow larger, if necessary.

Large crops such as squash, gourds, and melons hanging down from the vine will need extra support. You can make a sling out of an old t-shirt or swaddle them with some other material, such as this upcycled mesh produce bag.

Lightweight pea vines are perfect for growing on small supports, and they don't require much room in the garden. Pea plants are also frost-hardy, which makes them excellent early- and late-season crops. Use your vertical structure to keep plenty of space between the pea vines. The improved air circulation is good for them, plus it makes the pea pods easier to spot and pick.

PEAS

The smallest of the vining crops, peas are easy to grow and don't require much space to thrive. Though peas prefer growing in full sun, they will also grow well in a partially shady garden, which is great if you have a sun-challenged garden plot like I do.

Peas are a cool-season crop, which means that they can withstand frost in the spring and fall. This makes them the perfect candidate for growing two crops in the same season—one early and one late. Pea plants are pretty low-maintenance and don't usually have many problems with pests or diseases. (Watch out for hungry rabbits and deer though!)

Once you show them where the vertical support is, peas are good climbers, and their vining tendrils don't need much training. Be careful, though; the vines are very delicate and will break easily if mishandled. They are also lightweight and can be grown on small structures such as fan trellises or mini teepees made out of bamboo or twigs collected from your yard.

BENEFITS: Peas are cold-hardy and resistant to frost, so they can be planted much earlier than other crops, and, if timed right, they can be planted in late summer for a fall harvest. They are easy to grow and don't require any special care.

CHALLENGES: Rabbits and deer love peas, so the plants will need to be protected using some kind of barrier, such as wire fencing. Slugs can also be a problem during cool, wet weather, but they can easily be handpicked from the plants. Since peas are a cool-season crop, they will stop producing and die back once it gets hot in the summer.

PLANTING TIPS: Sow pea seeds directly into the garden in early spring four to six weeks before your average last frost date, and then again in late summer for a fall harvest.

SUPPORTS: Peas are terrific for growing on a smaller support, such as an obelisk, fan trellis, small teepee, or wire tomato cage.

POLE BEANS

A classic vegetable to grow, pole beans are probably the first vertical crop most people start with. Green beans are a staple for many gardeners, but there are other types of pole beans to choose from too, such as lima, asparagus, and runner beans.

Since the vines are so lightweight, pole beans can be grown on any type of vertical structure, as long as it's tall enough. Pole beans are also exceptional for covering larger structures such as arbors, arches, or pergolas.

The fast-growing vines can quickly cover a large structure, making an impressive statement in the garden. Pole beans are also an excellent choice for adding privacy or creating a screen to hide ugly walls or fences in your yard.

BENEFITS: Pole beans are easy to grow from seed, are heavy producers, and have vines that are very lightweight. They naturally grow vertically, and they will easily wrap themselves around any structure without much training. They are also fast-growing and will quickly cover any vertical structure.

CHALLENGES: Pole beans are loved by many types of pests and will need to be protected from four-legged creatures such as deer, rabbits, and voles. Slugs and Japanese beetles also tend to favor green beans.

PLANTING TIPS: Sow pole bean seeds directly into the garden after the last frost, once the soil has warmed up in the spring.

SUPPORTS: Pole bean vines grow very long, so be sure to use a support that is tall enough to give them plenty of space to grow. To ensure pole beans have plenty of height but still keep them within reach for easy harvesting, I like to grow my pole beans on arches, teepee structures, and tall trellises. They will also quickly cover a larger structure, such as an arbor or a pergola, but they can become difficult to harvest if the structure is too tall.

Pole beans, such as these Kentucky Wonders, are fast-growing vines that are perfect for climbing just about any vertical gardening support. They are excellent for adding structure and drama to the garden, creating private rooms, or using as a privacy screen.

Squash vines can be bullies. Growing them vertically keeps them from taking over the garden, and it also looks amazing. Mature vines get very heavy, so be sure to choose a strong, sturdy support.

SQUASH, GOURDS, AND PUMPKINS

One of the largest of the vining vegetables, squash plants when grown on the ground can quickly overtake a small garden plot. Growing squash vertically helps to keep this bully from taking over your vegetable garden, and it can look pretty amazing too.

Keep in mind that the vines of the largest varieties of squash (such as giant pumpkins and gourds) grow very long, and they may not be practical for vertical gardening. In fact, some grow so large that farmers have found pumpkins growing in the tops of trees!

Squash vines will become very heavy once the fruit starts to mature. So, if you plan to grow squash vertically, be sure to use a strong support for it. A large structure such as an arbor, arch, or pergola would be a good choice, but keep in mind that you may need to climb a ladder to reach your harvest.

BENEFITS: Squash plants are easy to grow from seed, and they are fast growers. Rabbits, deer, and other furry pests aren't usually a problem for prickly squash vines. The large vines will quickly cover a vertical structure.

CHALLENGES: Insect pests like squash borers and squash bugs can make it very difficult to grow squash plants, and powdery mildew can also be a major problem. Squash vines like to sprawl out horizontally rather than grow vertically, so the vines need to be trained regularly to grow on a vertical structure, or they can quickly take over the garden. Large squash that hangs down from the plant will need extra support so the weight doesn't damage the vine.

PLANTING TIPS: Wait until after frost once the soil has warmed in the spring, and then direct-sow squash seeds in a sunny location.

SUPPORTS: Squash vines need to be grown on large, strong supports that can handle their weight. Large structures such as heavy-duty arches, strong trellises, an arbor, or a pergola are good choices.

NON-CLIMBERS

Even if you don't have a large garden plot with tons of space for growing vining crops, you can still grow your favorite vegetables vertically. When we expand our growing space by adding vertical walls, living art, raised-bed planters, and other types of vertical container gardens, our options for what we can grow vertically are practically unlimited.

Non-climbing crops such as lettuce, herbs, and strawberries not only thrive in contained vertical growing structures; they look amazing too! Below is a list of non-climbing crops that would make excellent choices for growing in vertical container gardens.

LETTUCE AND OTHER GREENS

Greens—such as lettuce, spinach, arugula, swiss chard, and mache—can easily be grown in any size vertical container garden. These versatile crops come in a variety of sizes, and are great for adding tons of color to any garden.

Not only are they the perfect size for growing in vertical container gardens, but growing greens off the ground makes life much easier for gardeners who struggle with destructive ground-dwelling pests such as rabbits and slugs.

Plus, since you can put your vertical container garden anywhere, it's easy to provide a cool, shady spot that these heat-sensitive plants prefer. Greens don't like hot weather and are best when grown during the cooler spring and fall months, so keeping them in the shade can extend the harvest a bit longer.

BENEFITS: Greens are easy to grow, have minimal pest issues when grown vertically, and can be grown in any size vertical gardening container. Since they are frost-hardy, greens can be planted much earlier in the spring than heat-loving crops, and they can be planted again in late summer for a fall harvest.

Lettuce, herbs, and greens are not the first vegetables that leap to mind when you think of vertical gardening, but as long as you plant them so their weight does not uproot their delicate root structures, they will produce as well in a vertical environment as in a more traditional container.

CHALLENGES: Since greens are cool-season crops, the plants will bolt (flower and then produce seeds) as soon as it gets hot in the summer. Though greens grown vertically have fewer issues with pests, aphids can become a problem.

PLANTING TIPS: Direct-sow the seeds four to six weeks before last frost in early spring, or start seeds indoors earlier to get a jump start on the growing season.

CONTAINERS: Salad greens can thrive in any size vertical container garden. They are excellent for growing in vertical walls, gutter gardens, picture frames, and living art and are also fabulous fillers in tower gardens, hanging gardens, and planter boxes.

Herbs are versatile plants that are exceptional for growing vertically. They can be tucked into a mixed planting in a vertical wall or picture frame, or they can stand on their own in hanging baskets and stacked container gardens.

HERBS

Next time you visit your local garden center, take some time to peruse the herb section. If your garden center has a vast selection of herbs like mine does, you will be blown away by all of the different varieties available. I must confess, I'm currently obsessed with growing herbs. They come in so many different colors, sizes, and textures, and working with these delightfully fragrant plants is a pure joy.

Herb plants are very versatile and can be grown in any type of vertical container garden. They look as fantastic growing by themselves as they do when combined in mixed plantings. Many types of herbs are naturally pest-resistant, and some even work to deter pests from the garden.

Some types of herbs—for example, cilantro and dill—grow best during the cooler months and will bolt when the temperatures get too hot. Others, such as basil, prefer hot weather and will suffer in cool, wet conditions, so it's best to plant them at the same time as you plant warm-season crops such as tomatoes and melons.

Several types of herbs are perennial plants that can survive for many years (hardy varieties will vary depending on your growing zone), while others are annual plants that will only survive one growing season.

BENEFITS: Herbs provide a continual harvest, smell amazing, have many culinary and medicinal uses, are easy to preserve, and are really fun to grow. Most herbs have minimal pest issues, and some can even deter pests from munching on nearby plants.

CHALLENGES: Several types of herbs are prone to disease—especially in cool, damp conditions or when the plants have poor air circulation around their leaves—and most won't tolerate being overwatered. Some herbs, such as mint, lemon balm, chamomile, and oregano, can become quite invasive if planted in the ground and are best confined to growing in containers.

PLANTING TIPS: Some herbs are easier to grow from seed than others, so it's best to follow the instructions on the seed packet for each variety you plan to grow. Be sure your vertical gardening containers have adequate drainage to prevent overwatering.

CONTAINERS: Herbs are perfect for any type of vertical container garden and look especially amazing when used in vertical walls, gutter gardens, picture frames, and living art.

PATIO PLANTS AND BUSH VARIETIES

Bush varieties and patio plants are simply miniature versions of our favorite vegetables bred to thrive in small spaces or pots, and they are ideal for growing in many types of vertical container gardens.

These petite plants are wonderful for gardeners who want to grow vertically but don't have space for large vining crops, and there are more varieties to choose from on the market these days than ever before. When you go shopping, look for plants that are labeled as "patio," "container," or "bush" varieties.

You can find just about any type of your favorite vegetable plants—such as eggplant, peppers, okra, kale, or broccoli—in patio-sized varieties that will thrive in vertical container gardens. There are also bush varieties of many types of traditional vining crops; for example, tomatoes, beans, squash, cucumbers, peas, cane fruits, and melons.

BENEFITS: You can grow just about any type of your favorite vegetables even if you don't have a garden plot. Crops grown in pots have fewer issues with soil-borne diseases such as blight, and they require less overall maintenance than large vining crops.

CHALLENGES: Many types of patio plants and bush varieties are prone to the same ailments as their larger counterparts, and smaller plants usually produce smaller overall yields.

PLANTING TIPS: When deciding which varieties to grow in vertical container gardens, be sure to read the labels to find plants that will perform the best in your chosen container.

CONTAINERS: Patio plants and bush varieties are great for growing in tower gardens, hanging gardens, and medium to large sized vertical planters.

Peppers of most types make perfect patio plants and hanging gardens.

Edible flowers, such as these trailing nasturtiums, provide beauty and salad stock to your vertical garden.

EDIBLE FLOWERS

Edible flowers add tons of color and interest to vertical containers; they are a wonderful addition to any garden. They have the added benefit of attracting beneficial insects such as bees, which pollinate vegetables, and predatory insects that will fight to keep the bad bugs at bay.

Some common edible flowers, such as lavender, chamomile, and chives, fall under the category of herbs, while others, such as nasturtiums and pansies, are commonly grown as annual bedding plants. Edible flowers can be tucked into any vertical container garden, and they make superb companion plants for growing with vegetables.

Though there are tons of edible flowers that have a wide range of textures, flavors, and uses, not all flowers in the garden are edible, so it's important to research which flowers are safe to eat before you start snacking.

BENEFITS: Edible flowers add color and interest to vertical gardens and attract beneficial insects that will assist with pollination and insect pest control.

CHALLENGES: Edible flowers are best when harvested at their peak, which may only last a few hours for plants like squash—these flowers can only be harvested during a short window of time. Not all flowers are edible, so be sure you educate yourself on the types of flowers that are safe before eating any type of flower.

PLANTING TIPS: Some edible flowering plants (for example, nasturtiums) hate being transplanted, so the seeds should be sown directly in the garden. Follow the planting instructions on the seed packet or plant label for best results.

CONTAINERS: Edible flowers can easily be grown in just about any type of vertical container garden. Use them to add pops of color to tower gardens, planter boxes, hanging baskets, gutter gardens, vertical walls, and living art.

ROOT CROPS

Contrary to popular belief, root crops can indeed be grown in vertical container gardens, as long as the container is deep enough to allow for full growth of the roots and the plants aren't overcrowded.

Since they perform best in deep, loose soil that is free from impediments like rocks, twigs, and tree roots, many gardeners struggle to grow successful root crop harvests in the ground. In addition, voles, slugs, rabbits, and flea beetles can wreak havoc on root crops, which is another reason to grow them vertically instead.

Radishes and beets don't require as deep a container as carrots do, so make sure to do a little research about the plants you want to grow before planting root crops in your vertical vegetable garden.

BENEFITS: Root crops are frost-hardy, so they can be started much earlier than many other crops. When grown in vertical container gardens, root crops have fewer issues with pests, and it's easy to give them the precise mix of loose soil that they need to thrive and form beautiful crops.

CHALLENGES: Root crops, especially those with deep roots like carrots, won't produce well in shallow containers such as gutter gardens or vertical living walls, and will need to be grown in deep containers. Overcrowding can be an issue when root crops are grown in containers.

PLANTING TIPS: Root crops don't like to be transplanted, so it's best to direct-sow the seeds six to eight weeks before the last frost date and thin the seedlings if necessary for the best harvest. Root crops need adequate spacing to produce healthy crops, so take care not to overcrowd them.

CONTAINERS: Most root crops perform best when grown in deep containers, so stick to growing them in planter boxes, tower gardens, or stacked patio pots and containers.

Root crops such as these beets (mixed here with pansies), can be grown vertically as long as the container is deep enough for their roots.

STRAWBERRIES

Strawberries have shallow roots, which makes them sensational plants for growing in any type of vertical container garden. Most types of strawberry plants send out runners that, when grown vertically, will cascade down from the planter, adding a lovely decorative element to vertical container gardens.

Though they're easy to control, strawberry plants can quickly take over a small garden plot when planted in the ground. This makes growing them in vertical container gardens even more appealing. The runners will root themselves wherever they touch the soil, so you can simply lay them on top of the dirt to create new plants to fill in your vertical garden.

Growing strawberries in vertical container gardens also keeps them out of reach of hungry critters such as rabbits and voles, and strawberries grown in containers have fewer pest issues than those growing in the ground.

There are so many uses for strawberry plants in vertical gardening. You could create a vertical container garden specifically dedicated to growing strawberries, such as the strawberry tower project on page 173, or you could add them to mixed container plantings, where they will act as the "spiller" plant.

BENEFITS: Strawberries are easy to grow in shallow containers and, when grown vertically, have few issues with pests. Growing strawberries vertically makes it easy to keep the plants under control.

CHALLENGES: Container-grown strawberries can be killed during harsh winters if not given extra protection.

PLANTING TIPS: Plant strawberries in the spring while the temperatures are still cool. For best results, set the plant on top of the soil and cover only the roots, taking care not to cover the crown of the plant.

CONTAINERS: Strawberries are fantastic for growing in tower gardens, living walls, and hanging baskets, and they would be equally fabulous in gutter gardens, living picture frames, or planter boxes.

June-Bearing versus Everbearing Strawberries

Strawberry plants fall into two broad categories—June-bearing and everbearing. Both types of plants have the same growing requirements, and the main difference between them is the timing of fruit production and harvesting.

June-bearing: As the name would suggest, June-bearing strawberries produce fruit in late spring or early summer. Though they will only bear fruit once per year, the benefit of growing June-bearing strawberries is that they tend to produce larger fruit and higher overall yields than everbearing varieties.

Everbearing: Everbearing strawberries are also appropriately named, since they produce fruit throughout the entire growing season. With many varieties, the tradeoff is that everbearing fruits tend to be smaller, and the plants aren't as productive as June-bearing plants. However, new varieties of everbearing strawberries on the market these days have been bred to produce larger fruits and better harvests, giving everbearing strawberries even more appeal.

Don't worry—you don't have to choose one over the other. I grow both types of strawberry plants in my garden so that I can enjoy the benefits that each has to offer.

Strawberries don't require deep containers, which makes them ideal for growing vertically. The plants send out runners that cascade over the tops of vertical containers, adding a beautiful decorative element.

CARING FOR YOUR VERTICAL GARDEN

One of the biggest benefits of growing vegetables vertically is that it makes maintaining your vegetable garden much easier. Even though that's true, vertical gardens aren't completely maintenance-free. But with proper care, vertical gardening will help make it easier to keep your vegetable garden healthier and more productive, and you won't have to waste your entire summer lugging watering cans, pulling pesky weeds, or fighting pests and disease!

WATERING

Watering is one of the most important things to pay attention to when you're growing vegetables. If vegetables don't get enough water, they won't produce very much food. Whether your vertical garden is growing in the ground or on the patio or hanging on a wall, the same basic rules for watering vegetables apply.

Believe it or not, there is a right way to water plants and a wrong way to water plants. The correct way to water any vegetable garden is by directing the water at the base of each plant rather than over the tops of the leaves. When you water at the base, the leaves won't get wet. This prevents fungus and mildew growth. Watering plants at the base also helps to reduce weed growth in a vertical vegetable garden plot, because you're only watering the vegetables and not the entire garden (including all of the weeds).

It's also important to give your vegetables the correct amount of water. I know it sounds backward, but it's best to water your garden less often and with deeper waterings than it is to water it a little bit every day. If you water correctly with infrequent but deep waterings, the roots will grow deep, and the plants won't need to be watered as much. Frequent light waterings cause shallow roots, and plants with shallow roots will be dependent on you to water them more often.

Take special care when watering vegetables growing in planters and pots to ensure that there is adequate drainage to prevent overwatering.

When you have a big garden plot or a large collection of hanging planters and container gardens, watering can become a huge chore, especially during dry spells with little or no rainfall. The good news is that there are a few simple tricks that can ease the burden of watering your garden.

ABOVE: A drip irrigation system is easy to install in a vegetable garden plot or in any type of hanging vertical container garden, and it makes watering the garden a snap!

OPPOSITE TOP: Vining vegetable crops grown vertically can easily be protected from hungry rabbits by encircling the base of vulnerable plants with protective fencing.

OPPOSITE BOTTOM: Vertical vegetable gardens aren't completely maintenance-free, but with proper care, growing vertically will help make it easier to keep your vegetable garden healthier and more productive.

To train unruly climbing vines to grow on a support, gently weave or tuck the vines into and around the trellis. Take care not to force the vines as you train them, or they could break. Even plants with aggressive climbing tendrils will benefit from training.

One way to make the task of watering the vegetable garden easier is to add a layer of mulch over the soil. Mulching your garden has many benefits, and water retention is one of them. Mulch acts as an insulator so that the moisture is held in the soil and won't evaporate in the hot sun. You can add mulch over the soil of any type of vertical vegetable garden, including container gardens, to help the soil retain moisture.

Adding irrigation into your garden is a lifesaver when it comes to watering. You could simply weave soaker hoses through your vegetable garden plot, or take it a step further and install a drip irrigation system. Drip irrigation systems are quick to install in any type of vertical garden, and there are many kits available on the market to make it easy. Once it's installed, plug your DIY irrigation system into a garden hose timer to make watering your garden a snap.

TRAINING AND TYING

Many types of vining crops aren't great climbers on their own, so we have to give them a little bit of guidance and show them where we want them to grow. Some types of climbers will need to be tied to the support in order to grow vertically, while others will just need a little bit of training to guide them, and then they will grab on by themselves.

The fact that some vining crops have tendrils that will coil around anything they touch doesn't mean they will climb a structure all on their own. Gravity is fighting us, and many types of climbers are heavy and prefer to grow along the ground rather than climbing up a support.

It's easiest to train climbing plants when they are small and just beginning to vine out. For squash, cucumbers, and peas, you can gently weave the vines into the trellis or tie them onto the structure until they grab hold. Just be sure to tie them on very loosely—you don't want the ties to strangle or cut into the vines as they grow thicker. Once the tendrils clasp onto the trellis,

the ties can be removed and reused to tie new growth higher up on the support as the vines grow longer.

Crops that don't have tendrils or twining stems, such as tomatoes and raspberries, will need to remain tied to the support in order to stay in place. To train these plants, gently press the stem against the support, and tie it on loosely using twine, metal twist ties, or flexible plant ties. You can also buy plant clips that are made specifically for securing crops to vertical gardening supports.

Check on the vines every few days to train new growth as needed and to make sure they don't get off track and start growing on nearby plants instead of staying on their vertical support. Vining crops can be bullies in the garden!

WEED CONTROL

When you grow vegetables in vertical gardening structures such as wall pockets, towers, or living art, the struggle of dealing with weeds basically becomes nonexistent. But growing vegetables in the ground is a whole different ballgame. Controlling weeds in a vegetable garden plot is very important. Weeds compete with vegetable plants for water, light, and nutrients, and, if allowed to grow, they can quickly take over your vegetable garden—and your summer.

Weed control is one of the biggest struggles that gardeners face, and weeding the garden can end up becoming an overwhelming chore. Some even give up on gardening altogether because the weeds are incessant. But weeding the garden doesn't have to be so time-consuming if you take a few simple steps to keep weeds from growing in the first place.

A thick layer of mulch is the best way to prevent weeds from sprouting in your vegetable garden. Growing vining crops on trellises and other structures allows you to easily mulch around the base of each plant, which is a huge benefit of vertical gardening. For best results, add a 3- to 4-inch layer of mulch over the top of the soil. When adding mulch to the garden, avoid piling it around the stems of plants, as this could cause them to rot. Instead, keep the mulch about an inch away from the base of each plant.

In the vegetable garden, it's best to use lightweight mulches that will break down quickly and can be tilled or turned into the soil. Organic materials such as seed-free straw, chemical-free grass clippings, finely shredded wood, sawdust, pine needles, and leaves are all great choices (be sure to avoid using any part of the black walnut tree to mulch your garden though). These organic materials add nutrients to the soil as they break down, improving the soil quality and attracting worms. Apply mulch over the top of the soil liberally as needed throughout the gardening season.

For an added barrier against tough weeds, lay cardboard or a thick layer of newspaper over the top of the soil and wet it down before piling on the mulch. This will smother any existing weeds, giving you the upper hand.

Properly watering your vegetables will also help to discourage weeds from growing. Rather than watering the entire garden with a sprinkler, which waters the weeds too, focus the water directly at the base of each of the vegetable plants.

FERTILIZING

Feeding your vertical vegetable garden will give plants the boost they need to grow stronger and produce more food. Many types of vegetable and fruit plants are heavy feeders and will perform their best when they're fertilized regularly throughout the growing season.

This is especially important for vegetables growing in vertical gardens that are off the

ABOVE and OPPOSITE: A thick layer of mulch is the best defense against weed growth in the vegetable garden, and has the added benefit of feeding the soil. Use lightweight, natural mulches such as leaves or straw in a vegetable garden plot.

ground—such as living walls, hanging baskets, towers, and planter boxes—since they solely rely on us to provide the nutrients they need to survive.

When it comes to feeding your vertical vegetable garden, I recommend using natural organic fertilizers rather than synthetic chemical fertilizers. Chemical fertilizers give us instant gratification, but they cause major damage to the health and fertility of the soil over time. It's also much easier to burn the roots of plants with chemical fertilizers, which can damage or even kill the plant.

Organic amendments build up the soil over time, giving vegetables the rich, fertile soil that they need to thrive. When you use organic fertilizers, you're building up the soil structure to be a rich source of nutrients for your plants. Fertile soil means stronger, healthier plants, higher yields, and delicious organic food for us!

Using organic plant fertilizer in your garden shouldn't feel intimidating or make things more difficult for you. There are tons of wonderful options for natural fertilizers on the market, and these can be applied as a liquid or as slow-release granules that you add to the soil. For best results, be sure to follow the instructions on the fertilizer label.

DISEASE CONTROL

Many disease issues start at the soil level, so vertical gardens tend to have fewer problems with soil-borne diseases. Crops grown vertically also tend to have better air circulation around their leaves, which helps to prevent the spread of disease as well. However, at some point you will likely have to deal with some disease or fungus issues in your vertical garden.

Maintaining a healthy vegetable garden is the best way to prevent disease outbreaks. Proper watering, mulching, and pruning are all ways to keep problems like powdery mildew from ruining your crops.

One of the best defenses against disease outbreaks in your vertical vegetable garden is maintaining strong, healthy plants that will naturally be more disease-resistant. Plants that are stressed and weak are more vulnerable to disease.

It's also important to always pay attention to what's going on in your garden. As you go about your daily maintenance tasks, check for any signs of infection, such as discoloration or spots on the leaves. That way, as soon as you spot a blight-infected leaf or notice the first signs of powdery mildew, you can take swift action to get ahead of the problem before it spreads to the rest of your plants.

Pruning plants to allow for adequate airflow and making sure the foliage stays off the soil are two of the best ways to prevent disease and fungus issues. Mulching around the base of your plants prevents soil from splashing up on the leaves. This is a good way to prevent soil-borne diseases from infecting your plants.

Your watering routine can help prevent disease in your vegetable garden too. Watering plants in the morning so that the leaves can dry out during the day will help to slow down, or even stop, the spread of disease. If you water your garden in the evening, take care not to get any water on the leaves. That way they will stay dry overnight, which is another important preventive measure.

Another way to help control the spread of disease and keep your plants from being infected year after year is to make sure you never put diseased plant material into your compost bin. Instead, you should either toss the infected plant material into the trash or burn it to destroy the disease pathogens. Also, never reuse potting soil in containers or hanging gardens; it's important to always use fresh, clean potting soil when planting vertical gardens in any type of container or planter.

PEST CONTROL

For better or worse, bugs are a part of gardening. Back when I first started gardening, I absolutely hated the bugs! But guess what? Not all bugs are bad. In fact, many of the bugs you see in your garden, such as bees, wasps, and spiders, are actually beneficial insects. Once I started to learn about beneficial insects and how important they are for maintaining a healthy vegetable garden, I started to love the bugs—well, most of them anyway!

If you don't know much about the insects in your garden, I highly recommend you invest in a gardening book that's specifically about insects and learn how to identify the bugs in your garden. Once you understand the delicate balance of all those bugs out there and all the hard work the beneficial insects do for you every single day, it will definitely change the way you garden. Plus, when the bad bugs do show up, it's important to know your enemies so you can get rid of them quickly and efficiently.

But trust me; I get it. When the bad bugs are munching on your coveted vegetables, it's tempting to reach for the nearest pesticide spray to kill them all. Whatever you do, I implore you to stay away from using synthetic chemical pesticides. Chemical pesticides are not only bad for our health; they are also extremely toxic to the health of the environment and your garden. Organic pesticides are always the better option.

However, even organic pesticides shouldn't be the first thing you reach for when you discover a pest insect invasion in your vertical vegetable garden. Many insect pests can easily be controlled using physical methods such as handpicking, adding row covers, or simply knocking the pests off the plants with a strong spray of water from the garden hose.

If you're at wits' end and using a pesticide is your last remaining option, then look for natural and organic products that target only the pest insect, and never do any type of broad application of any pesticides in your garden.

It's important to use all types of pesticide, even organic ones, with extreme caution so you don't end up killing the good bugs in the process of trying to rid your garden of the destructive pests.

When it comes to furry pests—such as rabbits, voles, and deer—vertical gardens don't have as many problems as traditional vegetable gardens do, especially when you grow your food high above the ground and out of reach of those pesky four-legged critters. Vertical vegetable gardens growing in the ground can be protected by either encircling the base of vulnerable plants with protective fencing or building a fence around your entire vegetable plot.

Most types of pest insects, such as Japanese beetles, cabbage worms, and hornworms, can easily be controlled with physical methods such as handpicking or using row covers to protect the plants.

PRUNING AND PINCHING

Generally speaking, most vegetables don't need to be pruned at all, so you won't need to spend a lot of time pruning your vertical vegetable garden. But there are a few plants that benefit from being pruned once in a while, and there are other reasons why you might need to head to the garden armed with a sharp pair of pruners.

It's a good idea to get into the habit of checking your garden regularly and trimming off any dead or diseased leaves. This will keep your vertical gardens healthy and looking their best. Just be sure to disinfect your pruners by washing them with soapy water or dipping them in rubbing alcohol after trimming off any diseased material so you don't end up accidentally infecting other plants.

Plants such as tomatoes and herbs will benefit from being pruned or pinched regularly during the growing season. Not only does this promote healthy growth and lots of food production, it also improves air circulation, which helps prevent disease and fungus issues. Pinching the flowers off of basil and other herbs will also trigger new growth and extend your harvest.

Regular pruning and pinching keeps patio plants shapely and looking fabulous. Unruly vines can also be trimmed to control their size or in order to train them to grow over a wide structure rather than continuing to grow taller and longer.

Pruning also encourages vegetable plants to focus their energy on ripening the fruit. This trick is especially useful toward the end of summer when tomatoes and peppers are heavy with unripe fruit. Trimming the new foliage and pinching off the flowers will allow the plant to focus on ripening the fruit that's already on the plant, giving you a better late-season harvest.

Herbs and tomatoes look better and produce more food when pruned or pinched on a regular basis. Pruning also improves airflow and helps prevent the spread of disease.

Pruning Tomatoes

When I first became interested in gardening, I remember my dad telling me that if you remove the suckers from a tomato plant, you will get more tomatoes. I had no idea what he was talking about, so he patiently showed me what a sucker was and how to pinch it from the plant.

A sucker on a tomato plant is the extra growth that appears between the stem and a branch joint. If left to grow, a sucker will become another branch that can develop flowers, and even tomatoes.

The reason to remove these suckers is that they compete for the energy available to the plant. This extra growth can cause your tomatoes to be smaller, and overall tomato production could be lower.

Once you remove the suckers, your plant can dedicate more energy to producing tomatoes, rather than wasting energy on sucker growth. Suckers can also make a tomato plant look overgrown and cause it to become very heavy, so pinching them out on a regular basis allows you to control the size and shape of the plant.

Small suckers can easily be removed by pinching them out with your fingers. For larger suckers, it's best to cut them off with a sharp pair of pruners to avoid damaging the main stem.

While you're at it, it's a good habit to remove any yellowing leaves and leaves that are touching the ground to prevent blight and other soil-borne diseases. You can also prune off large leaves to further thin your tomato plant—this helps control the size and stimulates fruit production. Regularly pruning tomato plants results in higher yields, improves airflow, and prevents disease.

Regularly removing suckers—the extra growth between stem and branch—not only helps to keep tomato plants looking nice; it also allows the plant to dedicate more energy to producing yummy tomatoes.

Vertical gardening structures are not only functional; they can be used to add wonderful pops of color to the garden too. The bright blue obelisks and lattice trellises make this vegetable garden look stunning.

3

TRELLISES *and* OTHER STRUCTURES

PLANT SUPPORTS DON'T have to be purely functional; they can be beautiful too. When you start considering all of the different options you have for supporting your vining vegetable crops, it will really open your eyes to a whole new way of thinking.

One of the things I love the most about growing my vining vegetable crops vertically is that I can get so creative with it. Vertical plant supports add structure and beauty to the vegetable garden and give it a ton of character.

Most gardeners add plant supports to their vegetable gardens as an afterthought, out of pure necessity. Instead, I encourage you to think about how you can incorporate stunning vertical growing structures into your garden design before you even start planting your vegetable plot. Think of them as marvelous pieces of architecture in your garden, rather than necessary components you need to add as the plants grow larger.

When planning your vegetable garden, keep in mind that tall plant supports will cause shady spots in the garden. These shady nooks are excellent spots to plant small crops like lettuce and other leafy greens. Leafy crops and salad greens prefer a shady spot and will suffer when growing in the hot sun. You can also plant early crops, such as radishes and spinach, under tall structures, and they'll be harvested by the time the vining heat-loving crops fill in.

In this chapter, you will find the ideal plant support for any type of vining crop you want to grow. Whether you plan to grow lightweight vines such as pole beans, peas, or cucamelons; heavier crops such as cucumbers, gourds, and mini melons; or even the monster vines of grapes, squash, and hops, you'll find the perfect vertical gardening structure here.

There's a range of projects in this chapter, so if you're looking to build something a little more complex, try building an arbor, an obelisk, or a large trellis. If you're not good with power tools, don't worry; there are several projects here that don't require any complicated tools or special skills.

FREESTANDING ARBOR

An arbor is a classic vertical gardening structure that definitely deserves a spot in every garden. Adding an arbor can change the entire feel of your garden, and it will become a main focal point in the landscape. Arbors are fantastic for adding shade and privacy and are often used to create cozy nooks or secluded spaces in the garden.

Arbors are sturdy structures that can be used to grow the largest of the vining crops—squash, grapes, hops, or melons—but would look equally impressive covered by the thick vines of smaller climbers such as pole beans or cucumbers.

This version of the classic arbor design is a great size for any garden. It's large enough to command attention in big gardens, but not so large that it would overwhelm a small space. Put it over a path at the entrance of your yard or garden to welcome guests in, or use it to add shade to a sunny patio. This arbor would also be perfect for framing an area of your garden, or you could put a bench underneath it to create a quaint sitting area.

Just keep in mind that, since arbors are so tall, you will likely need to pull out a ladder each time you want to harvest the crops growing at the very tops of the vines.

MATERIALS:	TOOLS:
4 × 4 × 10' boards (4)	Drill
2 × 6 × 12' board (1)	⁹⁄₃₂" drill bit
2 × 6 × 8' boards (3)	½" socket wrench or drill adapter
1 × 2 × 8' boards (9)	Table saw
Carriage bolt ⅜" × 6", galvanized (8)	Miter saw
Washer & nut, galvanized, for bolts (8)	Tape measure
3" screws (4)	Hammer
1¼" finishing nails (64)	Pencil
2" finishing nails (56)	Eye and ear protection
	Work gloves
	Hammer or pneumatic nailer
	Square
	Ladder
	Posthole digger (optional if buried)

CUT LIST:

PART	DIMENSIONS	PIECES	MATERIAL
Sides, buried 2'	4 × 4 × 10'	4	4 × 4 × 10' board
Design on top structure	2 × 6 × 4'	6	2 × 6 × 8' board
Top of structure	2 × 6 × 6'	2	2 × 6 × 12' board
Vertical support for lattice	1 × 2 × 6'	4	1 × 2 × 8' board
Horizontal lattice pieces	1 × 2 × 19½"	16	1 × 2 × 8' board
Vertical lattice pieces	1 × 2 × 6'	4	1 × 2 × 8' board

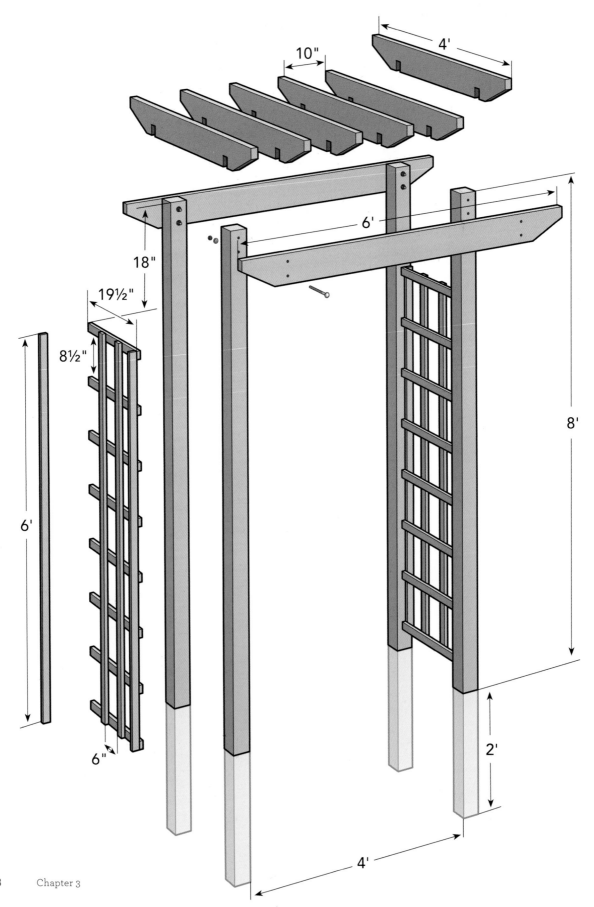

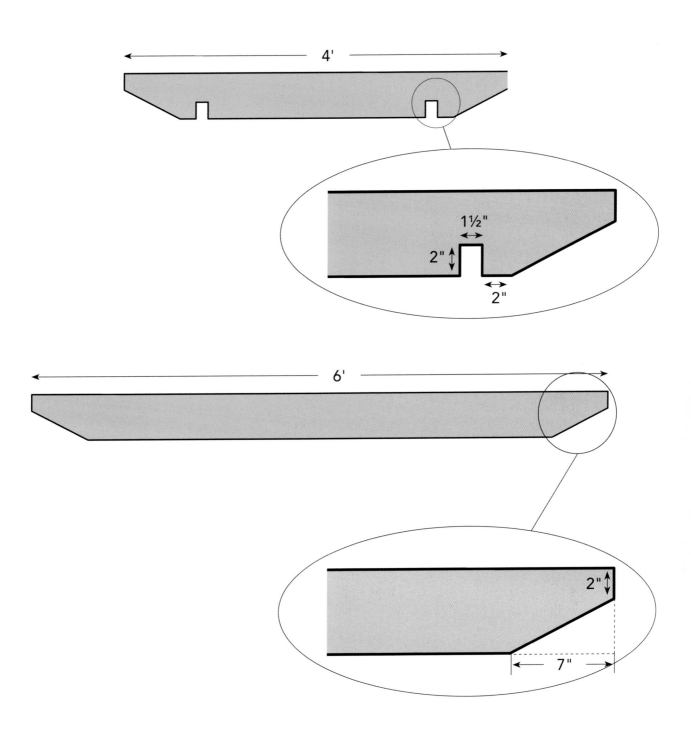

How to Build an Arbor

1

2

STEP 1: Measure and cut all of the lumber for the arbor using a miter saw. To cut angles in the decorative top boards, measure 2" down from the top corner of the board and make a mark, then measure 7" in from the bottom corner and make another mark. Draw a line to connect the two marks on the board, and use a table saw (or circular saw) to cut the angle. Secure workpiece to miter gauge. Repeat to cut angles in both ends of the 2 × 6 × 6' boards, and also in all six of the 2 × 6 × 3' boards. Once the angles are cut in the boards, take the six 3' boards and measure 2" in from the bottom of the angle to mark the spot for each of the notches. Cut two 1½"-wide by 2"-deep notches in each of the eight decorative top boards with a table saw.

STEP 2: Lay two of the 4 × 4 × 10' pieces of wood (the arbor legs) on a flat surface so they are parallel to each other and spaced 4' apart. Place one of the 2 × 6 × 6' boards perpendicular over the top of the legs. Ensure the top of the 6' board sits flush with the tops of the legs, and that it is centered, then use a ⁹⁄₃₂" drill bit to drill two holes all the way through both boards on each leg for the carriage bolts. Use a hammer to tap the carriage bolts through each of the pilot holes so they go all the way through both boards. Place one washer and one nut on the end of each bolt, and hand-tighten the nuts. Ensure the boards are square, and then use the socket wrench to tighten each of the bolts. Repeat step to assemble the other half of the arbor frame. Position each half of the arbor frame so that they are 19½" apart and sit parallel to each other, with the 6' boards on the top facing out. Use a posthole digger to dig holes that are 2' deep for each of the legs of the arbor, and place the arbor legs in the holes. Ensure that the two sides of the frame are completely level and sit at the same depth in the holes. You may need to make adjustments to the placement of the frame pieces, so don't bury the legs of the frame until after you have completed steps 3 and 4.

STEP 3: Starting at one end of the top board, slide a 4' board through the notches over the top board so it sits on the outside of the 4 × 4 frame legs. Ensure that the 4' board sits flush with both legs, and then drive 3" screws through the board to attach it to both legs.

STEP 4: Slide the rest of the 4' boards onto the top of the arbor, and space them so that they're 10" apart (the board on the end should sit on the outside of the arbor legs and be installed as explained in step 3). Secure the center boards to the top of the trellis by toenailing them using a pneumatic nailer or hammer.

STEP 5: Starting with one leg of the arbor, position one of the 1 × 2 × 6' vertical support pieces so that it's 18" down from the top of the leg and sits flush with the outside of the leg, then attach it to the leg using finishing nails. Repeat to install one vertical support piece onto each of the other three legs.

Tip:
To make the arbor more stable, pour concrete into the holes rather than burying the legs of the arbor with soil or gravel.

6

STEP 6: Starting on one side of the arbor, place one of the 1 × 2 × 19½" boards horizontal to the legs so that it sits flush with the top of both of the vertical support pieces. Attach each end of the horizontal piece to one of the vertical supports using nails. Repeat to install the remaining horizontal lattice pieces, spacing them 8½" apart. To install the vertical lattice pieces, position one of the 1 × 2 × 6' boards on the outside of the horizontal lattice pieces, spaced at 6" on center from the vertical support piece. Then attach it at each point where it crosses the horizontal lattice pieces using nails. Install the second vertical lattice piece so that it's 12" on center from the vertical support piece. Repeat step to install lattice on the other side of the arbor.

What Is a Pneumatic Nailer?

You will see a pneumatic nailer listed as one of the tools used for a couple of the projects in this book, and you might be wondering what the heck it is. A pneumatic nailer (also called a nail gun) is a tool that uses compressed air to drive nails into the wood, making the task much faster and easier.

Though you could use a regular hammer for building these projects, since there are a lot of nails required, a pneumatic nailer makes the job go much faster. It's certainly not required, but you might want to check to see if you can borrow one from a friend or neighbor or rent one for the day from a local hardware or home improvement store.

LARGE ARCH TUNNEL

Arches are one of my favorite vertical structures to use in my garden. Not only are they beautiful; they're functional too. Arches can provide a huge amount of growing space for vining crops.

This arch tunnel adds a magnificent architectural element to the garden and is perfect for growing large vining vegetable plants such as pole beans, melons, or squash. Use it to frame the entrance to your yard for dramatic appeal, or arch it over the top of a pathway to create shade and privacy.

The tunnel is made using 4-gauge wire fencing panels (also called cattle panels or livestock fencing), which can be found at any farm supply store. The metal fencing is very thick, and it makes a strong arch that can support large vining crops with ease.

One thing to keep in mind is that the fencing panels are very large (16 feet long), so plan accordingly when you go to pick them up. I learned this the hard way when we showed up with a pickup truck to haul away the fencing, only to find out the panel pieces wouldn't fit in the truck bed. We had to return later with a long trailer in order to bring them home.

MATERIALS:	TOOLS:
16' × 50" 4-gauge wire fencing pieces (3)	Hammer
9" heavy-duty metal landscape stakes (24) or tall fence post stakes (12)	Work gloves
	Eye protection

Note: The panel fencing pieces are heavy and very awkward to handle alone, so make sure you ask a friend to help you with this project.

How to Build a Large Arch Tunnel

STEP 1: Lay one of the fencing pieces on its side. Position one person at each end of the panel, and slowly walk toward each other to bend the panel into an arch shape. Stop when the ends of the panels are about 6' apart.

STEP 2: Slowly turn the arch so that it's standing up, then lift it into the garden and position it in the location where you want it.

STEP 3: Secure the bottom of the arch in the ground using four metal landscaping stakes on each side of the arch. Facing the tab of each stake toward the fencing, hammer the stakes into the ground at a slight angle. Once the landscaping stakes have been driven all the way into the ground, the metal tab of each stake should overlap the bottom piece of the fencing panel, ensuring that the panel is completely secured to the ground. Repeat steps 1 through 3 with the remaining two panels.

> **Note:**
> To stabilize the arches better, you could use 2' or 3' metal garden posts instead of landscaping stakes on the outside of the arches, and attach the fencing to the stakes using zip ties.

LARGE TEEPEE FORT

If you have kids, you know first-hand that it can be challenging to get them to eat their vegetables. Creating a special space for children in the garden is a wonderful way to get them interested in gardening, and also gets them excited about eating their vegetables. A large teepee fort is a fun place for kids to hide out, play, and grab a snack fresh from the vine whenever they want.

Pole beans are phenomenal for growing on a teepee fort. The fast-growing vines will quickly cover the teepee, and kids can easily pluck beans from the vine. To add more variety to the mix, you could interplant the pole beans with cucamelons or peas, which are also popular with the kiddos.

I used heavy-duty garden stakes for this project because I like how sturdy they are, and they will last a long time. These 8-foot-tall, heavy-duty garden stakes can be purchased at any garden center or home improvement store. Alternatively, you could use bamboo or even large tree branches if these materials are readily available to you. Just make sure they are 8 to 10 feet tall and sturdy enough to be driven into the ground.

MATERIALS:	TOOLS:
8' heavy-duty garden stakes (8)	Wire cutters
50' garden training wire	Ladder
	Work gloves
	Eye protection

How to Build a Large Teepee Fort

1

2

STEP 1: Space the poles about 1½' apart in a circle, leaving a 3'-wide space for the door, and angling the poles in slightly at the top toward the center of the circle. Then drive each one into the ground to secure it in place.

STEP 2: Standing on a ladder, gather the tops of all the poles together in the center of the circle, and secure them together 8 to 10" from the top of the poles using the garden training wire. Weave the wire in and out of the poles as you work your way around the grouping to ensure the tops of all the poles are secured together.

STEP 3: Run the rest of the wire around the entire outside of the teepee (leaving the space for the door open), wrapping it once around every couple of poles to secure it. Space the wire 10 to 12" apart as you work your way down the teepee. This will give the vines extra support and a place to grab on to as they grow so they can completely cover the teepee.

SMALL ARCH TRELLIS

By now you know that growing vining crops vertically is a huge space-saver. But guess what—using an arch trellis is a double space-saver! The best part about growing vines on a small arch like this is that you can grow shorter crops such as lettuce, carrots, or herbs underneath it, giving you twice the space in your garden!

This small arch trellis is an ideal size for any garden and is perfect for growing cucumbers, cucamelons, or other smaller vining crops. The rebar pieces make the arch very strong, so it will have no problem supporting the weight of a vine full of mature cucumbers or mini melons.

Another benefit of growing vining crops on this small arch is that the vegetables will hang down, making them easy to see. The arch is also tall enough that you won't have to bend over too far to harvest.

Once the fencing has been secured onto the rebar frame, the arch is portable too. Simply pull the rebar pieces out of the ground, move the arch to the new spot, and push the rebar back into the ground.

MATERIALS:	TOOLS:
10' pieces of ⅜" rebar (2)	Wire cutters
28" 16-gauge metal garden fencing	Scissors
8" cable zip ties (12)	Work gloves (rebar is messy, so I recommend using gloves whenever you're handling it)
	Eye protection

Note: It is difficult to get the two rebar arch pieces into the exact same shape, so get them as close as you can. They don't need to be exactly the same, since they will be spaced apart in the garden.

How to Build a Small Arch Trellis

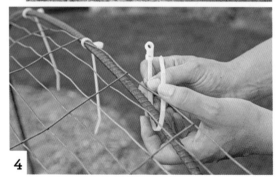

STEP 1: Carefully bend each of the ⅜" rebar pieces into arches. The rebar will bend pretty easily, but take your time bending it because if you force it, the rebar could kink. You are aiming for an arch with 4' of space.

STEP 2: Install the arch pieces in the garden by driving the ends of the rebar into the ground. Space the ends of each arch 4' apart and the arches themselves 28" apart.

STEP 3: Lay the garden fencing over the top of the arch to measure how long the piece should be cut. Use wire cutters to cut the fencing to size.

STEP 4: Secure the fencing to the rebar arches using the zip ties, spacing the zip ties every 6 to 10" along the entire length of the rebar. Cut the extra tabs off the zip ties using scissors, if desired.

Using Garden Fencing for Trellising Large Vegetables

If you're using a trellis made out of garden fencing, chicken wire, or a similar type of material that has small holes in it, you'll need to keep an eye on your squash, melons, and cucumbers.

Baby vegetables can easily grow through the holes, and they sometimes get stuck in the fencing as they grow larger. So be sure to watch out for all of the new vegetables as they start to grow, and move them out of the holes before they grow large enough to become stuck in the fencing.

Don't worry; if you do find one that's become wedged in the fencing, you can still harvest it. Simply take a sharp knife and cut the fruit in half so that you will be able to remove it from the fencing. You can still enjoy your harvest; this just means you'll have to eat that one right away.

CLASSIC OBELISK

Traditionally found in formal gardens, obelisks are fancy plant supports that have four sides and a pyramid-shaped top. In ancient times, obelisks were impressive structures made of stone. But these days, garden obelisks are usually made out of wood or metal.

Obelisks are stunning in the garden, and I am a bit obsessed with them. They are fabulous and elegant features that add lots of interest as well as structure to the garden, and they can be very artistic too. Garden obelisks can be found in a wide range of shapes and sizes, and they look just as good without anything growing on them as they do covered with vining crops.

This version of the classic obelisk is 6 feet tall and extremely sturdy. Set it in a level spot, or sink it a few inches into the ground to ensure that it's stable, and then use it to grow vining crops such as cucamelons, cucumbers, small gourds, or mini melons.

Let the wood age naturally to give the classic obelisk a more rustic feel, or paint the wood to keep the formal look and add extra color to the vegetable garden. To make it even more classic, you could always add a decorative finial on the top.

MATERIALS:	TOOLS:
2 × 2 × 8' boards (4)	Drill
1 × 2 × 8' boards (5)	Table saw
#8 × 1¼" screws (44)	Ladder
#8 × 2" screws (4)	Eye and ear protection
Wood post cap (1)	Work gloves
	Tape measure
	Pencil

CUT LIST:			
PART	DIMENSIONS	PIECES	MATERIAL
Legs	2 × 2 × 6'	4	2 × 2 board
Bottom horizontal bands (outside)*	1 × 2 × 22½"	2	1 × 2 board
Bottom horizontal bands (inside)*	1 × 2 × 21"	2	1 × 2 board
Second horizontal bands (outside)*	1 × 2 × 17"	2	1 × 2 board
Second horizontal bands (inside)*	1 × 2 × 15½"	2	1 × 2 board
Third horizontal bands (outside)*	1 × 2 × 12"	2	1 × 2 board
Third horizontal bands (inside)*	1 × 2 × 10½"	2	1 × 2 board
Fourth horizontal bands (outside)*	1 × 2 × 7"	2	1 × 2 board
Fourth horizontal bands (inside)*	1 × 2 × 5¼"	2	1 × 2 board
Center decorative pieces	1 × 2 × 4'	4	1 × 2 board

ANGLE ON DECORATIVE PIECE:	ANGLE ON BANDS:
45 degrees on top	11.5 degrees

* All measurements are prior to the angle—they are the longest point of the wood piece.

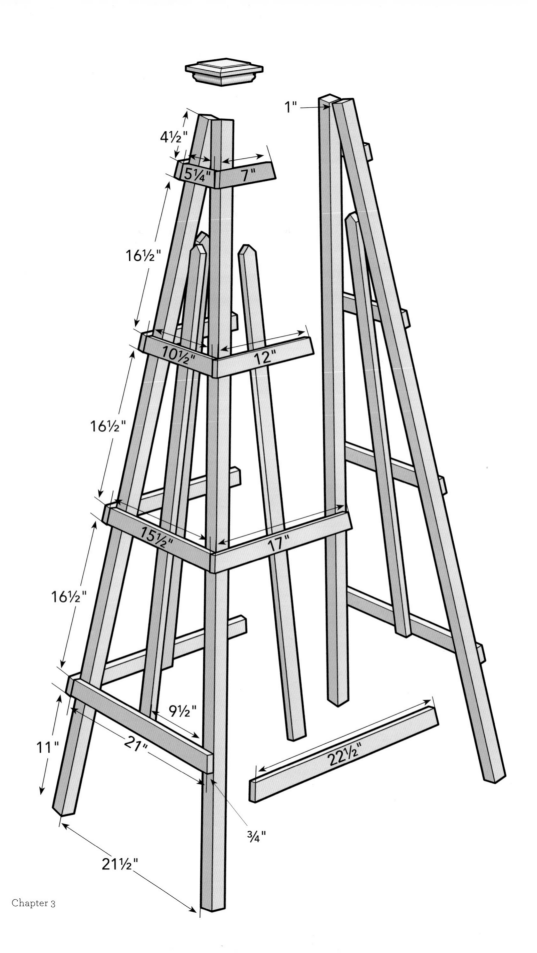

4½"

1"

5¼"   7"

16½"

10½"   12"

16½"

15½"   17"

16½"

9½"

11"   21"

22½"

¾"

21½"

How to Build a Classic Obelisk

STEP 1: Measure and cut the wood for the obelisk using a miter saw, and then cut 11.5-degree angles at both ends of each of the bands. Use a miter saw to cut two 45-degree angles at one end of each of the four vertical decorative pieces, creating a point.

STEP 2: Lay two of the 2 × 2 leg pieces down on a flat surface. Angle them so that the tops of the two leg pieces are spaced 1" apart and the bottoms are spaced 21½" apart. Position one of the 21" bands 11" up from the bottom of the legs, and lay it across the 2 × 2s. Ensure that the band is straight and that the angled ends of in the band are flush with the outsides of each of the legs. Predrill pilot holes through each end of the band into of the legs. Drive one 1¼" screw into each of the pilot holes to secure the band to both of the legs. Position one of the 15½" bands 16½" up from the top of the first band, and repeat the steps to secure the band to the legs. Repeat again to secure one of the 10½" bands and then one of the 5¼" bands to the legs, each spaced 16½" apart. Repeat step 2 to assemble the other half of the obelisk.

3

4

5

STEP 3: To attach the two sides of the obelisk together, stand both sides up and position them so that they are leaning into each other (the bands should be facing out). Angle the two pieces so that the tops are spaced 1" apart and the bottoms are spaced 21½" apart. Position one of the 22½" outside bands so that it sits parallel to the bottom bands on both halves of the obelisk, and the ends of each band are lined up with the ends of the bands that are already attached to the obelisk. The outside band should overlap the legs by ¾" to line up with the inside bands. Predrill pilot holes through each end of the outside band into both of the legs, and drive one 1¼" screw into each hole to attach the band to both legs.

STEP 4: Working from the top of the obelisk to the bottom, follow the instructions in step 3 to attach the remaining three outside bands to the obelisk, starting with the 7" band at the top, then the 12" band, and finally the 17" band. Carefully flip the obelisk over and repeat steps 3 and 4 to secure the fourth side.

STEP 5: Stand the obelisk on its feet and place the cap over the top of all four 2 × 2s. Predrill pilot holes through the top cap and into each of the 2 × 2s, then drive a 2" screw into each pilot hole to secure the top cap to the obelisk.

STEP 6: Starting with one side of the obelisk, position one of the vertical decorative pieces so that it is centered between the legs on the inside of the horizontal bands. The flat end of the decorative piece should be lined up with the bottom edge of the longest horizontal band (the bottom band), and the pointed end of the decorative piece should be facing up. Ensure the decorative piece is centered and straight, then predrill pilot holes through each of the three horizontal bands into the vertical decorative piece, and drive one 1¼" screw into each of the pilot holes to attach the vertical decorative piece to the frame. Repeat step to attach the remaining three decorative pieces to the frame.

CONTEMPORARY OBELISK

Obelisks are one of my favorite vertical gardening structures. Not only are they great to use for growing vining crops; they add a unique and decorative touch to the garden too. Though I adore the classic obelisk design, I wanted to come up with a fresh design for modern garden spaces. So for this project, I put my own contemporary spin on the classic obelisk form.

The silver metal pipes and steel hardware give this obelisk a sleek, industrial feel that I love. Silver looks terrific against bare wood, but it would really pop if the legs of the obelisk were painted or stained using a darker color. To make this contemporary obelisk your own, add a fancy finial on top, or use a decorative cap rather than the simple wood one that I use here.

This small obelisk looked amazing covered by pea vines in my garden. Other small vining crops, such as cucumbers or miniature melons, would work equally well growing on this snazzy obelisk.

MATERIALS:	TOOLS:
2 × 2 × 8' boards (2)	Circular saw or handsaw
10' electrical metallic tubing (EMT) conduit (1)	Drill
5' EMT conduit (you will only need 2½' of it, so buy a shorter length if you can) (1)	⅛" drill bit for pilot holes
	Pipe cutter
½" 2-hole EMT straps (20)	Tape measure
#8 × ⅜" sheet metal screws (40)	Pencil
2" screws (4)	Eye and ear protection
Wood post cap (1)	Work gloves

CUT LIST:			
PART	DIMENSIONS	PIECES	MATERIAL
Legs	2 × 2 × 4'	4	2 × 2 board
Crossbar	17½"	2	EMT conduit
Crossbar	15"	2	EMT conduit
Crossbar	12½"	2	EMT conduit
Crossbar	15¾"	2	EMT conduit
Crossbar	13½"	2	EMT conduit

Note: Before you begin assembling your obelisk, take a moment to pop one pipe strap onto each end of all ten pipe pieces (the end of the pipe should be flush with the outside edge of the pipe strap). This will keep the pipes from rolling away as you work, and will also make assembly a little faster.

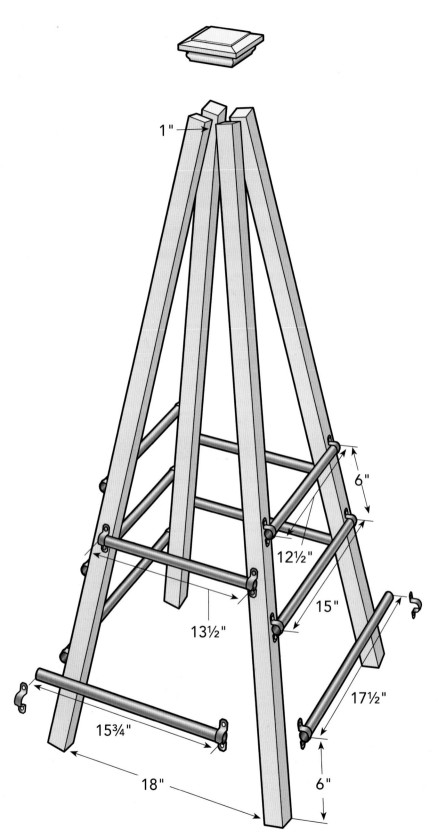

1"

6"

12½"

15"

13½"

17½"

15¾"

18"

6"

How to Build a Contemporary Obelisk

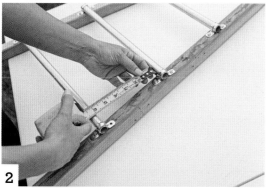

STEP 1: Lay two of the 2 × 2 pieces of wood on a flat surface. Angle them so that the tops of the two pieces are spaced 1" apart and the bottoms are spaced 18" apart. Position one of the 17½" EMT pieces 6" up from the bottom of the 2 × 2s, and lay it across the 2 × 2s. Ensure that the pipe straps are centered on each 2 × 2, then predrill pilot holes into the wood through each hole in the pipe straps. Drive one sheet metal screw into each pilot hole to secure the conduit to both of the 2 × 2s. Ensure the screws are tight enough to firmly hold the pipe in place.

STEP 2: Position one of the 15" pipes 6" up from the 17½" pipe. Repeat step 1 to attach the pipe to the 2 × 2s. Then repeat step 1 again to attach one of the 12½" pipes 6" up from the 15" pipe. Repeat steps 1 and 2 to assemble the other half of the obelisk.

STEP 3: To attach the two sides of the obelisk together, stand them up and position them so that they are facing in opposite directions (the pipes should be facing out). Angle the two pieces so that the tops are 1" apart and the bottoms are 18" apart. Position one 13½" pipe so it's centered on the 2 × 2s between the top two pipes. Predrill the pilot holes and secure the pipe to the 2 × 2s using the sheet metal screws. Then position the 15¾" pipe so it's centered between the bottom two pipes, and attach it to the 2 × 2s. Flip the obelisk over and repeat step 3 to secure the other side.

STEP 4: To attach the top cap, stand the obelisk on its feet and place the cap over the top of all four 2 × 2s. Predrill pilot holes through the top cap and into the 2 × 2s, then drive a 2" screw into each pilot hole to secure the top cap to the obelisk.

LARGE TRELLIS

Trellises come in lots of different shapes and sizes and are easy to find for sale at any garden center or home improvement store. But for the handy DIYer, it's just as easy to build your own. If you're looking for a classy trellis that will hold loads of vertical crops, then this one is for you.

The inspiration for this project came out of the need for filling a large space in my garden. I have a 10-foot-long raised bed that is right next to the side of the house. The huge blank wall above the bed was boring to look at, and I wanted to utilize that wasted space to grow more food. A dainty trellis wouldn't do—I needed something more substantial to cover the area—so this large trellis was designed to take up space.

This sturdy trellis would make a wonderful support for tall vines such as pole beans, cucamelons, or cucumbers. It's perfect to use as a screen to hide an unattractive fence or shed, or to cover a boring blank wall like mine; it could even double as a privacy wall next to a patio or sitting area in the garden. To cover even more space, build a few of these trellises and then line them up side by side to quickly cover an expansive area of the garden.

MATERIALS:	TOOLS:
2 × 2 × 8' boards (6)	Drill
1 × 2 × 8' boards (5)	Miter saw
#8 × 1¼" screws (5)	Pencil
#8 × 2" screws (5)	Tape measure
1¼" finishing nails (48)	Work gloves
	Hammer or pneumatic nailer
	Rubber mallet
	Level
	Eye and ear protection

CUT LIST:

PART	DIMENSIONS	PIECES	MATERIAL
Vertical frame pieces	2 × 2 × 7'	5	2 × 2 board
Top of trellis frame	2 × 2 × 4'	1	2 × 2 board
Bottom of trellis frame	1 × 2 × 4'	1	1 × 2 board
Inside diamonds	1 × 2 × 15¾" at longest point	12	1 × 2 board
Outside edge diamonds	1 × 2 × 14¼" at longest point	12	1 × 2 board

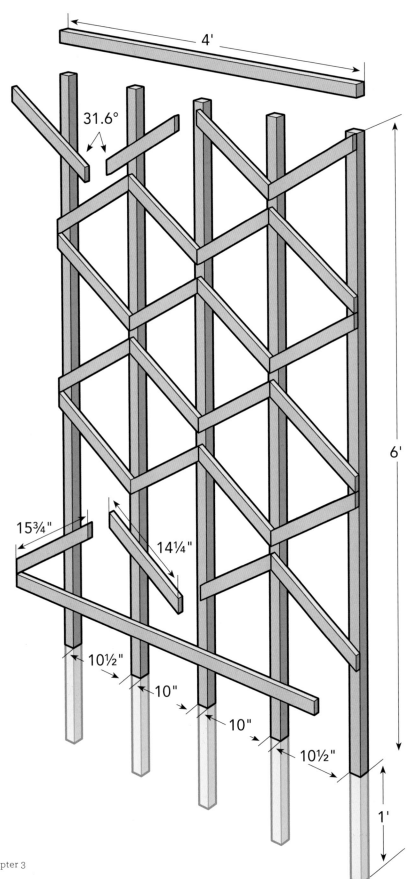

How to Build a Large Trellis

STEP 1: Measure the length for each of the pieces of the diamond pattern. Set the appropriate angle on the miter saw, and cut the opposite corners of each angle piece at 31.6 degrees.

STEP 2: Lay the frame pieces of the trellis frame down on a flat surface. The five 7' pieces should be laid parallel to each other with a 10" space between the inside boards, and a 10½" space between the outside boards. Place the 2 × 2 × 4' board perpendicular to the top of the 7' boards. Ensure the frame is square, predrill pilot holes in the top frame piece, and attach the boards together using 2" screws. Lay the 1 × 2 × 4' board perpendicularly across the 7' boards, 2' from the bottom of the trellis. Predrill pilot holes, and attach the 4' board to the frame using the 1¼" screws.

STEP 3: Leave the assembled frame flat on the ground, and lay out the diamond pattern over the top of the frame. Use the 15¾" angle pieces to create the pattern on the outside edges of each side of the frame, and use the 14¼" pieces to create the diamond pattern at the top and in the middle of the frame.

STEP 4: Use a hammer or a pneumatic nailer to attach the diamond pattern to the frame, ensuring that it is secure at every point where each of the pattern pieces crosses the trellis frame.

STEP 5: To install the trellis in the garden, use a shovel to dig a hole at least 1' deep for each leg. Set the legs of the trellis in the holes and ensure that the trellis is level before burying the legs with dirt. Use a rubber mallet to gently tap the top of the trellis until it is level, if necessary.

UPCYCLED GARDEN TOOL FAN TRELLIS

A fan trellis is a timeless and classic design that adds form and function to the garden. There's a wide variety of materials that can be used to build a fan trellis, but what better material to use than gardening tools? This upcycled garden tool fan trellis puts a fun spin on the classic fan trellis design. Not only would it be an adorable addition to any garden; it's a great conversation starter too.

This project gives rusty or broken old gardening tools new life. You can use any type of long-handled garden tools that you want. Use old hoes, rakes, shovels . . . whatever you have available to you. Inexpensive old garden tools are easy to find at yard sales, antique markets, or even your local thrift store.

Using round wood extension poles, which can be found at any home improvement store, as the crossbars mimics the shape of the handles on the garden tools. It won't take long for the wood to age and blend right in with the aged look of the garden tool handles. Even better, you could use the broken handles of other old garden tools as the crossbars instead.

MATERIALS:		TOOLS:	
Old wooden long-handled garden tools of your choice (3)		Tape measure	
¼" × 3" machine screws (9)		Drill	
60" wood extension poles (or upcycled handles from old garden tools) (2)		¼" drill bit (for drilling bolt holes)	
		Circular saw or handsaw	
		Pliers	
		Pencil	
		Eye and ear protection	
		Work gloves	

CUT LIST: *			
PART	DIMENSIONS	PIECES	MATERIAL
Top crossbar	34"	1	Wood extension pole
Center crossbar	28½"	1	Wood extension pole
Bottom crossbar	23"	1	Wood extension pole

* Depending on the types of gardening tools you use, you may need to make your crossbars longer or shorter. I cut mine to allow a 3" overlap on each side of the trellis.

How to Build an Upcycled Garden Tool Fan Trellis

STEP 1: Before cutting the extension poles for the crossbars, lay out your trellis pattern on the ground. Space the tools evenly, and then measure the space between them to determine the exact length of your crossbars. Cut the crossbars.

STEP 2: After cutting the crossbars, lay out your trellis pattern again, putting the garden tools over the top of the crossbars. Mark the three spots on each tool handle where it overlaps one of the crossbars. This is where you will drill the pilot holes for the bolts.

STEP 3: Drill pilot holes at each point that you marked in step 2. Each hole should be drilled all the way through both the tool handle and the crossbar.

STEP 4: Drive the bolts through the pilot holes so they go all the way through both the tool handle and the crossbar. At this point, the trellis will be very loosely attached together.

STEP 5: Carefully turn the trellis over, and hand-tighten one nut onto the end of each of the bolts. Ensure the trellis is straight, and then use the pliers to tighten each of the bolts until the trellis is completely secure.

PIPE FAN TRELLIS

A pipe fan trellis may sound complicated, but this design is extremely easy to build using common materials that can be found at any home improvement store. It's also a very inexpensive project, which is fantastic, especially if you need to build several trellises for your garden.

If you're looking for a versatile trellis, this one is the perfect size for use along the side of a house, shed, or fence, or it could be added to a raised garden bed. The size is just right for vining crops such as peas and cucumbers and is equally useful for supporting your tomato plants.

This simple fan trellis design looks great as is, or it could be painted to give it even more character. Stain or paint the wood crossbars using a bold, dark color for a striking contrast against the silver pipes. Or spray the entire trellis with bright paint to add a fun pop of color to your garden.

MATERIALS:	TOOLS:
10'-long ½" EMT conduit (2)	Saw
1 × 2 × 8' board (1)	Tape measure
½" 2-hole EMT straps (15)	Pipe cutter
#8 × ⅜" sheet metal screws (30)	Drill and drill bit
	Pencil
	Eye and ear protection
	Work gloves

CUT LIST:			
PART	DIMENSIONS	PIECES	MATERIAL
Long vertical bars	5'	2	EMT conduit
Short vertical bars	40"	3	EMT conduit
Top crossbar	1 × 2 × 3'	1	1 × 2 board
Middle crossbar	1 × 2 × 2½'	1	1 × 2 board
Bottom crossbar	1 × 2 × 2'	1	1 × 2 board

Cutting Metal Pipes

Don't be intimidated by the thought of cutting metal pipes or worried that you'll have to buy an expensive piece of equipment to get the job done. A simple pipe-cutting tool is inexpensive to buy and will work great for any of the projects in this book.

Clamp the pipe onto a workbench or table to hold it in place for easier cutting. Support the end of the pipe with a sawhorse (or have a friend hold it for you) while you make the cuts.

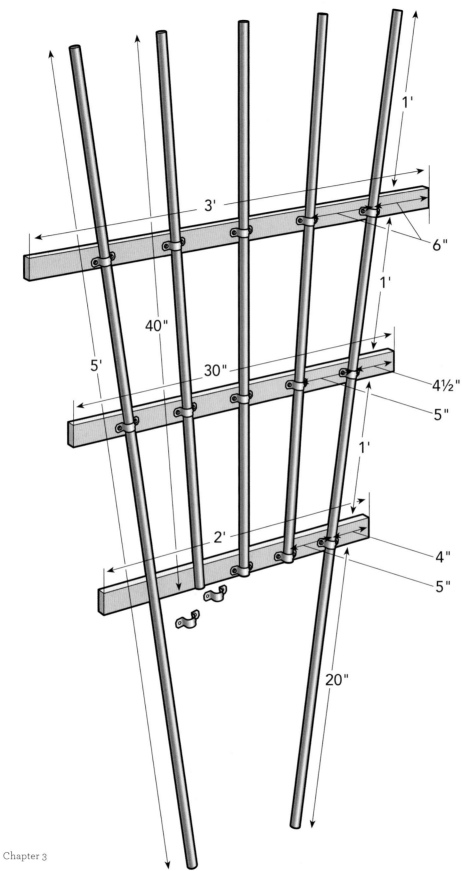

How to Build a Pipe Fan Trellis

STEP 1: Measure the lengths of pipe, and then use the pipe cutter to cut them to size. EMT conduit is fairly thick, so you may need to clamp the pipe down to your table or workbench to hold it in place in order to cut it.

STEP 2: Measure and cut the wood for the horizontal crossbars.

STEP 3: Measure and mark the places on the wood crossbars where the pipes will cross.

STEP 4: Starting in the center of the trellis, line up one of the 40" pipes vertically over the marks you made on the crossbars. Pop a pipe strap onto the pipe, centering it over the crossbar. Drill pilot holes into the wood through the holes in the pipe strap. Drive sheet metal screws into the pilot holes to secure the pipe onto the crossbar.

STEP 5: Repeat step 4 with the remaining pipes, securing each of the pipe straps tightly to ensure the trellis is completely secure.

Tip:
For the three shortest pipes, start with securing the pipe strap at the bottom of the trellis, and work your way up. The bottom of each of the three shorter pipes should sit flush over the bottom crossbar.

COPPER TRELLIS

Copper is a wonderful material to work with, and it looks gorgeous in the garden too. This trellis was designed to take up lots of space and add privacy to a backyard sitting area or patio. I designed this trellis to look beautiful not only when it's covered in vines but also while standing on its own during the off-season.

The copper pipe frame creates a sturdy base, and this trellis is big enough to handle larger crops such as pole beans, cucumbers, or squash. Once you build the frame, you could leave it as is, or add a pattern to it as I did here. Follow the instructions to use my pattern design, or use your creativity to come up with your own design.

Keep in mind that copper will naturally develop a patina as it ages, so your shiny copper trellis will eventually turn brown, and then green, over time. Of course, this isn't a bad thing. Patinated copper is the look everyone is striving for these days—meaning your DIY copper trellis will eventually make your neighbors green with patina envy.

MATERIALS:	TOOLS:
10' long ½" copper pipes (3)	Pipe cutter
½" copper 90-degree elbow connectors (2)	Super glue (Gorilla Glue® is recommended)
½" copper tee connectors (7)	Cable-cutting tool
50' 6AWG solid bare copper wire	Pliers
18-gauge copper wire	Wire cutters
Zip ties (optional)	Tape measure
	Work gloves
	Eye protection

CUT LIST (PIPES FOR FRAME):			
PART	DIMENSIONS	PIECES	MATERIAL
Vertical bars	16"	6	Copper pipe
Legs	2'	3	Copper pipe
Top and middle horizontal bars	4'	3	Copper pipe
Bottom horizontal bars	23¾"	2	Copper pipe

CUT LIST (WIRE FOR PATTERN): *			
PART	DIMENSIONS	PIECES	MATERIAL
Ovals	50"	8	Bare copper wire
Long lines	20"	9	Bare copper wire
Short lines	10"	2	Bare copper wire

* If you decide you want to design your own pattern, then the lengths and sizes of bare wire will vary. You will need less bare wire for a simpler pattern, but you may need more bare wire depending on how intricate your pattern design is. Sketch out your design ideas on paper before cutting any of the bare wire.

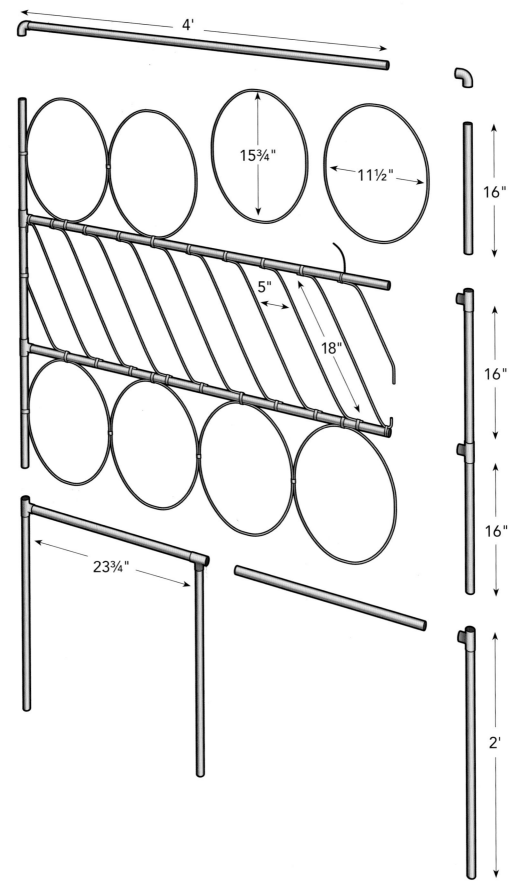

4'

15¾"

11½"

16"

5"

18"

16"

16"

23¾"

2'

How to Build a Copper Trellis

STEP 1: Use a pipe cutter to cut the copper pipes to size. Copper is a very soft metal, and it's fairly easy to cut the pipe without any extra help. However, you may find it easier to clamp the pipe to a table or workbench to hold it in place as you're cutting it.

STEP 2: Lay the pipes for the frame flat on the ground, and assemble all the pipes together using the pipe connectors. The connectors will slide easily onto the ends of the pipes, and most of them will fit very loosely.

STEP 3: To tightly secure the frame together, glue the connectors onto each of the pipes. After adding the glue to the end of the pipe, press the pipe firmly into the connector to ensure a tight hold. Allow the glue to dry completely before moving the frame.

STEP 4: Cut the bare wire pieces using a cable-cutting tool, then lay out the pattern and mark the frame for placement. To attach the straight pieces to the frame, use pliers to create a 1" bend at each end of each of the 20" straight bare wire pieces so the bends line up with the frame. To create the oval pieces, wrap the bare wire around a five-gallon bucket or similar object to make smoother bends. Use zip ties to temporarily attach your entire pattern to the frame before moving on to step 5. This will make it easier to wrap the pieces with wire and glue the pattern onto the frame.

STEP 5: Attach the entire design to the frame using the 18-gauge wire at each point where the pattern touches the frame. Once your pattern is fully secured with the copper wire, dab some glue over the copper wire and the bare wire to adhere your design securely on the frame. Allow the glue to dry completely before moving the trellis.

Whether you're looking to dress up a boring blank wall or fence in your yard, or you don't have a yard at all and are limited to gardening in a small space, you will find tons of inspiration in this chapter to let your imagination run wild.

4

LIVING WALLS
and
HANGING GARDENS

VINING CROPS ARE fantastic, but they limit our options for growing vertically to only a handful of vegetables. When you start adding vertical walls, living art, and hanging gardens into the mix, your options for what you can grow vertically are almost unlimited.

Small non-vining crops, such as greens, herbs, strawberries, and edible flowers, can flourish in just about any size container and are terrific for growing in these types of vertical gardens.

Hanging gardens, especially living art and vertical walls, have become very popular ways to grow succulents and other ornamental plants—but they are also a wonderful way to grow food! These innovative vertical gardens are especially great for those who have a small growing space, or wannabe gardeners who don't have a yard at all and are limited to gardening on a balcony, patio, porch, or deck.

You can display these projects just about anywhere, and not only will you be able to grow food in places you never considered before; it will look amazing too. Plus, being so high off the ground means that these gardens will be safe from pesky rabbits and other hungry ground-dwelling creatures.

Whether you're looking to dress up a boring blank wall or fence in your yard or you want to add some bright and unique living art to your garden, deck, or patio, this is the chapter for you! From vertical walls to edible living art and stunning hanging gardens, you will find tons of inspiration in this chapter to let your imagination run wild. These projects are meant to inspire your creativity and encourage you to experiment with unconventional methods for growing your own food in a style that's all your own. It's time to think outside the box of traditional vertical gardening and add some flair and personality to your growing space.

UPCYCLED LIVING PICTURE FRAME

Picture frames are no longer just for displaying photos of our loved ones or favorite works of art. Living picture frames have become a very popular trend these days, and this project is a great way to upcycle old frames.

Picture frames come in tons of different shapes and sizes, and it's fun to mix and match a few of them to create a decorative element on a blank wall or fence in your yard. You can even paint the frames to add bold splashes of color to your garden as I did here.

Used picture frames are a dime a dozen at secondhand stores and garage sales and are very easy to find. Or maybe you have a bunch of old ones collecting dust in storage that you can—literally!—give new life to. Wherever you find them, be sure to choose square or rectangular picture frames that are at least 1½ inches wide for this project. The wider the frame, the easier it will be to work with, and the better it will look in the garden.

MATERIALS:	TOOLS:
Upcycled picture frame	Drill
1 × 4" board	Wire cutters
Hardware wire mesh	Tape measure
Landscaping fabric	Circular saw or handsaw
Spray paint (optional)	Fabric shears
¼" × 1" deck screws (8)	¹⁄₁₆" and ³⁄₃₂" drill bits
⅜" staples	Staple gun
1½" finishing nails (4)	Hammer
Small D-ring hangers	Work gloves
30-lb hanging wire	Eye and ear protection
Soilless potting mix (see page 137)	Soil scoop or trowel

MY FRAME DIMENSIONS:	
INSIDE	OUTSIDE
7½" × 9½"	10¼" × 12¼"

CUT LIST:			
PART	DIMENSIONS	PIECES	MATERIAL
Short side of box	1 × 4 × 8"	2	1 × 4 board
Long side of box	1 × 4 × 11½"	2	1 × 4 board

Note: Remove the backing and glass and any staples or nails from the picture frame before starting.

How to Build an Upcycled Living Picture Frame

STEP 1: Spray paint the premade frame (or build your own and then paint it) and allow it to dry completely while you work on the next steps.

STEP 2: Line up the wood pieces to form a box (with the shorter pieces inside of the longer pieces). Ensure the box is square, then drill ³⁄₃₂" pilot holes and join the box parts with deck screws.

STEP 3: Square the wire mesh over the box, and cut it to size using wire cutters. The wire mesh should be slightly smaller than the perimeter of your box (rather than overhanging the edge) to avoid any sharp edges.

STEP 4: Before stapling the wire mesh onto the box, add a layer of landscaping fabric to hold the soil in the box. Lay the landscaping fabric over the box so it overlaps by a few inches on each side of the box. Overlapping the landscaping fabric (rather than cutting it to size first) makes it easier to staple everything together. Line up the cut wire mesh piece so it's square on top of the box, then staple the mesh and landscaping fabric onto the box.

STEP 5: Using the fabric shears or a pair of sharp scissors, trim off the extra landscaping fabric all the way around the box.

STEP 6: Flip the box over, and fill it completely with the soilless potting mix, pressing the soil down firmly into the box as you fill it. Once the box is completely filled with soil, repeat steps 4 and 5 to cover this side of the box with landscaping fabric and mesh, stapling them onto the box.

STEP 7: Line up the picture frame squarely on top of the box, and ensure it's centered. Drill ¹⁄₁₆" pilot holes, then attach the frame to the underlying box with finishing nails.

STEP 8: To plant your living picture frame, use wire cutters to make a small hole in the wire mesh for each plant, then use scissors to cut slits corresponding in the landscaping fabric. Use your fingers to loosen the dirt, and gently press each rootball into the soil. Add more soil into the hole if necessary to hold the plants in place. Wait a few weeks for the plants to become established before hanging your living picture frames.

Tips:
- Once the frame is attached to the box, you can use the spray paint to cover the nailheads, and also to touch up any accidental hammer dings in the frame.
- To water a living picture frame, take the frame off the wall and lay it flat to give it a good soaking. Allow the water to soak into the soil and drain completely before hanging the frame back up again.

Make as many
individual frames
as you wish, then
plant them and
arrange them on
a fence or wall.

Spray Painting Tips

Spray paint is a wonderful way to add extra splashes of color throughout your garden and give upcycled living picture frames or other vertical gardening projects your own special touch. Here are a few tips for spray painting your picture frame:

When choosing spray paint for your project, be sure you buy the right paint. Some types of spray paint won't stick to plastic or metal, so check the label on the can before purchasing the paint.

Always wear eye protection when using spray paint. Latex gloves are optional but work great for keeping your hands protected from paint overspray.

Make sure the surface of your project is clean and dry before spraying it with paint. Spray paint won't stick if there's grease or oil on your project.

Plan to spray paint your project on a day when there's no wind, or spray it in a well-ventilated area that is protected from the wind.

To paint the Living Picture Frame, lay it on a flat surface and place it on top of a piece of cardboard or thick layer of newspaper to protect the area under the frame from the paint overspray.

When spraying your picture frame, be sure to hold the can at least 12 inches away from the frame, and make steady, even strokes over the entire frame. It's best to spray several thin layers of paint rather than trying to cover the picture frame with one heavy coat of paint. Holding the can too close or spraying too thick a layer will cause the paint to run or look uneven.

If your frame has raised designs on it, spray the paint from several different angles to ensure full coverage of all the nooks and crannies of the picture frame.

LARGE SELF-STANDING LIVING ART

Using an easel is a fabulous way to display the most treasured piece of artwork in your home, so why not make one for your garden and use it to display an amazing piece of edible living art! This project combines art and function to create a unique piece of living art that will grow and change over time, so your artwork will never stay the same for very long.

Place this gorgeous piece of art standing at the entrance of a path or gate as a fun way to welcome guests into the garden. Or use it to liven up a boring corner of your patio or deck, creating an interesting conversation piece that will look different every time guests come back to visit.

Be sure to choose a colorful selection of plants with contrasting shapes, heights, and sizes to make your living art really pop. The more variety you use, the more interesting your living art will be.

Oh, and if you don't like the look of the chicken wire fencing inside the frame, don't worry, it's totally optional. In fact; it wasn't even part of my original design—I decided to add it to the frame after I had already planted everything. I like how it gives my taller plants extra support, and adding it also meant I could pop in a few small vining crops to add even more height to my living art. (I tossed in a couple of pea plants and trained some chocolate mint to climb the chicken wire too!)

MATERIALS:	TOOLS:
2 × 3 × 6' boards (3)	Drill
2 × 6 × 7" board (1)	⅛" drill bit for pilot holes
24" wooden planter box (1)	Table saw
Large picture frame (1) (the outer dimensions of my frame are 30½" wide × 26½" tall)	Miter saw
21" chain (1)	Eye and ear protection
3½" door hinge kit (1)	Work gloves
#8 × 2" screws (7)	Tape measure
#8 × 1¼" screws (13)	Pencil
Chicken wire fencing (optional)	Staple gun (if adding optional chicken wire fencing)
Spray paint (optional)	Wire cutters (if adding optional chicken wire fencing)
Soilless potting mix (see page 137)	Soil scoop or trowel

CUT LIST:			
PART	DIMENSIONS	PIECES	MATERIAL
Easel frame legs	2 × 3 × 6'	3	2 × 3 board
Easel frame crossboard	2 × 3 × 2'	1	2 × 3 board
Top bracket	2 × 6 × 7"	1	2 × 6 board

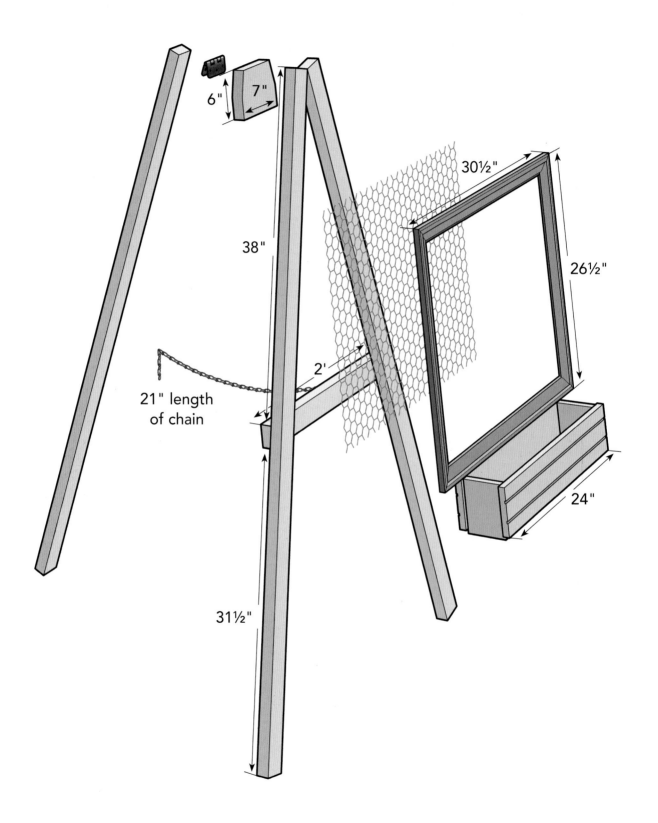

6"

7"

30½"

38"

26½"

2'

21" length
of chain

24"

31½"

How to Build Large Self-Standing Living Art

STEP 1: Lay two of the 6' boards down on a flat surface. Angle them so that the tops of the two boards are touching and the bottoms are spaced 36½" apart. Align the top bracket piece over the 6' boards (legs) so that it is level and centered at the top of the legs. Mark the bracket piece with the angle of the two legs, then cut angles in the top bracket to match the angles of the legs. Line the bracket piece up over the tops of the legs again, then predrill pilot holes through the top bracket and into the legs. Drive a 2" screw through each pilot hole to attach the top bracket to both of the legs.

STEP 2: Measure 38" from the top of each of the two 6' boards and mark the spot where the 2' crossboard will go. Ensure the crossboard sits level and is centered over the legs. Predrill a pilot hole through the 2' board into each of the 6' boards, then drive a 2" screw into each pilot hole to attach the crossboard to the legs.

STEP 3: Lay the third 6' board (the third leg) down at the top of the frame so that one end of the third leg is centered between the top boards of the frame. Lay the hinge flat, and place one half over the third leg, and the other half over the bracket on the frame. Drill pilot holes through the holes in the hinge into the 6' board, and also into the top bracket on the frame. Drive 1¼" screws through each hole to attach the hinge to the third leg, and use 2" screws to attach the hinge to the frame.

4

STEP 4: Drill a pilot hole in the center of the crossboard, and then drive a 1¼" screw through one end of the chain to attach it to the crossbar. Stand the easel up on all three legs, then space the third leg so that it's directly across from the center of the crossbar. Drill a pilot hole into the third leg, and then drive a 1¼" screw through the other end of the chain into the pilot hole to attach the chain to the third leg.

STEP 5: Center the planter box directly over the top of the crossboard. Drill two pilot holes through the planter box into each of the two front legs of the easel frame, then drive 1¼" screws through the pilot holes to attach the planter box onto the easel.

5

STEP 6: Place the picture frame on top of the planter box, and ensure it's centered on the easel. Drill four pilot holes through the frame into the legs at each point where the picture frame crosses the legs of the easel. Drive 1¼" screws through the pilot holes to attach the picture frame to the easel.

6

Note:

If you want to paint the picture frame, you can paint it before attaching it to the easel, or you can wait until it's fully assembled to paint it. If you want to add the chicken wire fencing on your frame, do it before attaching the frame to the easel. To install chicken wire, lay the picture frame face down on a flat surface. Lay the chicken wire fencing over the back of the frame, and cut it to size. Then use a staple gun to attach the chicken wire fencing to the back of the frame.

Where Should You Put Your Planter?

There are so many fantastic places you could display your living art, vertical walls, and hanging gardens, but you can't just thoughtlessly place them anywhere. There are a few things to consider when looking for the perfect spot.

The first thing to figure out is how much light the area will receive. Think about the plants you're growing and how much light those plants will need before hanging your vertical garden or displaying your living art.

Most small non-vining crops will grow just fine in partial shade. Lettuce, leafy greens, and some types of herbs will suffer if they are exposed to the hot afternoon sun and actually grow better in a shadier location. Plus, the soil in vertical hanging gardens will dry out much faster when it's hanging in the full sun.

Another thing to consider when choosing the best place to display your vertical garden is how much water it will get when it rains. Vertical gardens hanging under the eaves of a house or sitting directly below large trees could be protected from the rain and therefore remain dry after a rainfall, which means you'll have to water them more often.

I recommend displaying your vertical garden in a place that gets morning and/or evening sunlight but is protected from the intense afternoon sun. An open area where the garden will be watered when it rains is ideal, but a protected spot that is shaded from the blazing afternoon sun will work as well, as long as you remember to water the garden regularly.

Your easel can be placed just about anywhere in your garden. While direct sunlight is usually best for veggies, look for a spot with partial shade.

ANTIQUE LADDER HANGING PLANTER

Antique ladders have become popular pieces of interior decor used by savvy designers to create everything from rustic bookshelves to shabby chic bathroom towel racks. Since it's such a popular trend, I wanted to use an antique ladder to create a cute and functional vertical garden. But since they are so popular, real antique ladders can be difficult to come by—so let's build our own!

This replica antique ladder planter is very easy to build, and inexpensive too. It looks adorable sitting on the front porch or leaning against an old garden shed or fence. If you're lucky enough to own an antique ladder, you can definitely use it instead of building your own.

For this project, I used simple metal buckets that I found at a local department store, and I hung them from the ladder using large S hooks. To make your ladder planter look even more authentic, you could comb local antique shops for buckets or basket planters to hang on it instead.

It won't take long for the wood to age, making the ladder look more authentic. But, if you prefer to speed up the process, you can use simple painting and distressing techniques to make the ladder look like it's been sitting in your garden for years.

MATERIALS:	TOOLS:
2 × 4 × 8' board (2)	Drill
1" × 4' wooden dowels (3)	1" chisel bit
Wood glue	⅛" drill bit for pilot holes
#8 × 2" screws (10)	Miter saw
Hanging planters*	Eye and ear protection
2¾" S hooks (14) (optional, if your planters don't have hooks built in)	Work gloves
	Tape measure
Soilless potting mix (see page 137)	Pencil
	Hammer or rubber mallet
	Wood clamps

CUT LIST:			
PART	DIMENSIONS	PIECES	MATERIAL
Side of the ladder	2 × 4 × 6'	2	2 × 4 board
Rungs	20"	5	Wooden dowels

* The maximum width of the baskets/buckets should be 17". I used 3 large buckets (5⅛" tall × 14⅝" wide) and 4 small buckets (5⅛" tall × 5⅛" wide).

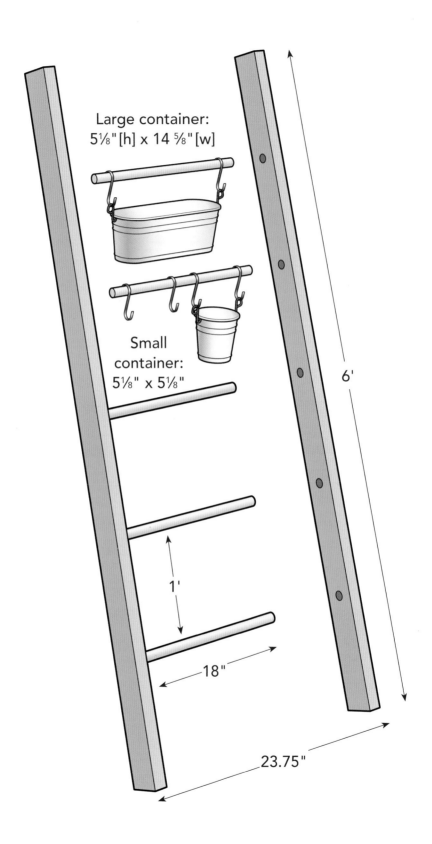

Large container:
$5\frac{1}{8}$" [h] x $14\frac{5}{8}$" [w]

Small
container:
$5\frac{1}{8}$" x $5\frac{1}{8}$"

6'

1'

18"

23.75"

How to Build an Antique Ladder Hanging Planter

STEP 1: Lay the 6' boards on a flat surface. Stretch the tape measure along the length of the 4" surface of one board, then make a mark every 1' along the entire length of the board (five marks total). Repeat with the second 6' board.

STEP 2: At each mark on the board, use a 1" chisel bit to bore a 1"-deep hole into the center of the board. Repeat with the other board.

STEP 3: Put wood glue into each of the rung holes on both of the 6' boards.

STEP 4: Press one end of a wooden dowel into each of the holes on one of the 6' boards. Use a hammer or rubber mallet to drive the dowels all the way into each of the holes. Lay the other 6' board with the holes facing down over the top of the dowels. Line up the rung holes on the second board with the dowels, then press the ends of the dowels into the holes in the second board or tap them in with a rubber mallet.

Why Use Wood Glue?

You'll see wood glue used in a few projects throughout this book, and you might be wondering why it's used for some projects but not others. Wood glue is a very strong adhesive that works great for gluing pieces of wood together. However, wood glue alone is not strong enough to attach the wood permanently for the projects in this book. The projects that call for wood glue are ones that will be holding a lot of weight. Adding wood glue before driving in the screws or adding extra support makes the bond much stronger, so your project will last for years to come.

STEP 5: Carefully lay the ladder down flat, and then clamp the two sides together on the outside of the legs using wood clamps. Tighten the wood clamps to press the dowels all the way into each of the rung holes, ensuring a tight fit.

STEP 6: Predrill pilot holes through each leg of the ladder into the ends of each of the dowels. Then drive a screw into each of the pilot holes to reinforce the ladder rungs. Allow the glue to dry completely before moving the ladder.

STEP 7: Drill drainage holes into the bottom of each of your hanging planters, if they don't already have them. Then use the S hooks to hang the planters, ensuring each planter or set of planters is centered on the ladder rungs.

The ladder rungs function as hangers, so you can use them to support any kind of container you wish, including hanging planters of all shapes.

HANGING CONE PLANTERS

When I was a kid, making May Day baskets was one of my favorite things to do in the spring. Our May Day baskets were cute little cones that we made out of construction paper, tape, and glue. After meticulously decorating our special baskets, we added pipe cleaner handles, filled them with candy, and sneakily hung them on the doors of unsuspecting neighbors.

This project was inspired by my fond memories of May Day baskets. I love how these hanging cone planters move and spin in the wind, and the longer you make the twine, the more they will move. They are perfect for dangling under a deck or pergola, from the ceiling of a porch, or from the branches of large trees.

I chose to use burlap to line the baskets for this project because I really like the soft look the fabric creates and the way it bunches over the top of the planters, softening the hard edges of the wire mesh cones. Burlap can be found at most garden centers, as well as home improvement or fabric stores. If you don't like working with burlap, you could use coconut liners or landscaping fabric to line your cone planters instead.

Come to think of it . . . maybe I should create more of these adorable cone planters to hang on the doors of unsuspecting neighbors. That would be an excellent way to give away extra plants!

MATERIALS:	TOOLS:
Wire mesh	Wire cutters
Burlap	Scissors
Twine	Needlenose pliers
Soilless potting mix (see page 137)	Tape measure
Wire ties (optional)	Work gloves
	Eye protection
	Soil scoop or trowel

CUT LIST:
12" × 12" wire mesh piece for small cone
16" × 16" wire mesh piece for large cone
32" × 16" burlap piece for small cone
44" × 22" burlap piece for large cone

How to Make Hanging Cone Planters

STEP 1: Use wire cutters to cut the wire mesh to size, leaving the wire tabs long on one end so that you can use them to secure the cone together. Cut the burlap to size, and then fold it in half the long way to create a double layer. Lay the cut piece of wire mesh on a flat surface and position the burlap over it so that the fabric overhangs the edge of the mesh at the top of the cone and is square with the bottom point of the cone.

STEP 2: Bend the mesh into a cone shape, tucking the ends of the burlap into the cone as you work. Go slowly as you create the cone shape so you don't make any kinks in the mesh.

STEP 3: Use the needlenose pliers to bend the overlapping tabs of wire mesh, and attach the sides of the cone together. Be sure to secure the cone down the entire length of the seam so it won't pop open. Use optional wire ties if necessary to secure the cone together.

STEP 4: Cut the twine to the desired length for hanging, and tie one end of the twine to each side of the cone at the top. Ensure the twine is centered so that the cone hangs level.

Planting cones
can be made in
many ways with
many materials.
These are simple
wire mesh frames
lined with burlap.

SIMPLE VERTICAL WALL POCKETS

Vertical wall pockets are a brilliant way to add life to a boring fence or blank wall, and they don't have to be complicated to make. When I found a set of inexpensive hanging baskets at a local discount store, the inspiration for this project was born. These simple vertical wall pockets are ideal for any small space and look darling hanging on a fence or adorning the railing of a deck or balcony.

The baskets I found were made for hanging on the insides of cabinet doors, so they already had hooks on them. But if your baskets don't have built-in hooks, you could use large S hooks to chain them together like I did, or simply hang each basket separately on a nail.

I lined my baskets with a thin layer of sheet moss, which can be found at many garden centers, as well as home improvement and craft stores. The sheet moss adds a lovely decorative touch but doesn't hold the soil in very well on its own, so I lined the inside of the sheet moss with landscaping fabric to contain the soil. Alternatively, you could skip the sheet moss and use landscaping fabric by itself, or you could line your baskets with burlap or coconut liners if you prefer.

These charming vertical wall pockets are nice for growing small edible plants such as herbs, strawberries, or salad greens. Be sure to hang them near your kitchen door to make it easy to pop outside and snip off the exact amount of herbs you need in your recipes or whip up a quick salad using fresh salad greens.

MATERIALS:	TOOLS:
Decorative wire baskets (3)	Fabric shears
Sheet moss	Soil scoop or trowel
Landscaping fabric	Work gloves
S hooks (6) (optional, if your baskets don't have hooks built in)	
Soilless potting mix (see page 137)	

Watering a Hanging Vertical Garden

Rainwater alone may not be enough to keep hanging vertical gardens evenly watered. The top tiers of a living wall or stacked hanging planters can shield the lower levels from receiving any rainwater. Or, in the case of living picture frames, the rainwater can run off so quickly that it doesn't have a chance to soak in at all, leaving the soil dry even after a heavy rainfall. When watering a vertical wall or hanging planters, be sure to water each pocket and planter individually so that every tier of the garden is watered evenly.

How to Make Simple Vertical Wall Pockets

1

2

3

STEP 1: Start by lining the inside of one of the baskets with sheet moss.

STEP 2: Next, line the inside of the sheet moss with a small piece of landscaping fabric—this will help to keep the soil in the basket. Press the landscaping fabric into all four corners and smooth it along the inside of the basket to remove any bunching. Use the fabric shears to trim off any excess fabric that overlaps the top of the basket.

STEP 3: Fill the planter with soilless potting mix and add your plants. The number of plants you use in each basket will depend on the size of your baskets. Repeat steps 1 through 3 with the remaining two baskets before hanging your simple vertical wall pockets.

DIY Soilless Potting Mix Recipe

When growing food in vertical gardens that are hanging on a wall, fence, or other structure, choose a lightweight soilless potting mix like the one in my recipe below. The soilless mix will gain weight when saturated with water, but it will be much lighter than regular potting soil.

Supplies needed:
A measuring container*
Shovel or trowel
Large container for mixing
Water (if the ingredients you're
    using are dry)

Soilless potting mix recipe:
2 parts peat moss or pre-moistened
    coconut coir
Garden lime**
½ part perlite
¼ to ½ part vermiculite

* I use a 1-gallon bucket, but you can use any size measuring container you want.
** Peat moss is acidic, and most vegetables and herbs prefer a more alkaline soil. So, if you use peat moss, you should add 1 tablespoon of garden lime per gallon of peat moss to your potting mix to balance out the acidity level. On the other hand, if you're growing plants that prefer an acidic soil (like berry plants), then don't add any garden lime to your mix.

Instructions:
Pour all of the ingredients into a large container, and use a shovel or trowel to stir it together until well mixed. Add water as you stir if your ingredients are extremely dry. Once everything is thoroughly mixed together, your potting soil can be used right away. Be sure to store any unused potting mix in a sealed container to keep bugs out.

DIY LIVING VERTICAL WALL

The first time I laid eyes on a large-scale vertical wall garden, my heart skipped a beat, and I instantly fell in love with the idea. From that moment on, I knew I just HAD to figure out a way to build one in my garden someday.

Living walls make gorgeous additions to the garden, and they are a wonderful way to grow your own food. Creating a living wall garden opens up your growing options, allowing you to utilize an area of your yard where you otherwise couldn't grow anything. Vertical wall gardens also make harvesting easier, putting your crops right at eye-level. No bending required! Plus they keep your crops out of reach of pests that plague traditional vegetable gardens.

While dedicating an entire wall or fence to building a massive vertical wall garden would be awesome, it's not practical for most people—including me. So I wanted to come up with a scaled-down version of a vertical garden wall that anyone could build. This DIY living vertical wall can be mounted on an exterior wall or fence and is perfect for growing strawberries, herbs, or salad greens.

The pockets are made out of heavy-duty landscaping fabric, but you could use thick felt or similar fabric if it's readily available to you. Just be sure to buy the strongest fabric you can find (I used 25-year landscaping fabric). Once filled with soil and water, the pockets will get very heavy, and thin fabric won't hold the weight of the wet soil.

MATERIALS:	TOOLS:
½" plywood, 24 × 48" (1)	Table saw
3' 25-year landscaping fabric	Paintbrush or roller (if painting the board)
⅜" staples	Staple gun
Exterior latex paint (optional)	Straight edge
100-lb. hanging wire	Tape measure
Large D-ring hangers (2)	Fabric shears
Soilless potting mix (see page 137)	Marker or pencil
	Wire cutters
	Drill
	Eye and ear protection
	Work gloves
	Soil scoop or trowel

CUT LIST:			
PART	DIMENSIONS	PIECES	MATERIAL
Fabric pockets	3' × 21"	4	Landscaping fabric
Pocket reinforcers	2 × 4"	8	Landscaping fabric
Board	24 × 48"	1	Plywood

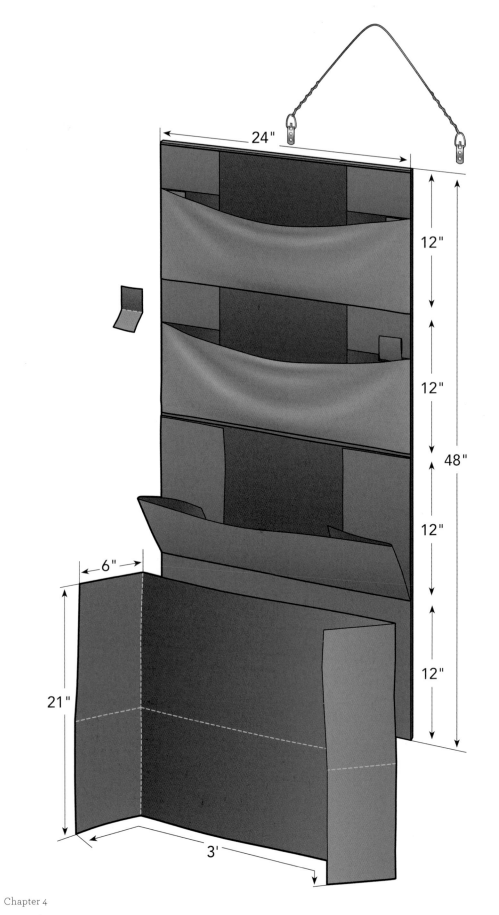

Caring for Vertical Living Walls

There's no doubt that growing food in unusual hanging vertical gardens like these is a fun trend, but caring for plants hanging on a wall or fence has its challenges, and watering is the main one.

The soil in hanging gardens will dry out much faster than it does in planters and containers sitting on the ground, so these gardens will likely need to be watered more often. It's also important to water vertical gardens thoroughly to ensure that all of the plants are being evenly watered.

If, after growing your vertical hanging garden for a season or two, you find that watering is too much work and the planters are drying out too quickly, try lining them with plastic before planting next time.

Adding a plastic liner will help to keep the soil from drying out so quickly and should make it easier to keep your gardens evenly watered. Just be sure to poke a few drainage holes in the plastic before planting.

Installing an inexpensive drip irrigation system will also help to keep your plants perfectly hydrated without any extra work from you.

SELF-STANDING PRIVACY WALL GARDEN

One of the many possible uses of vertical growing is to create a privacy screen, and that is the inspiration for this project. For gardeners who live in close proximity to their neighbors, it's nice to be able to create an outdoor space where you can read a book or enjoy your morning coffee without feeling like everyone is watching. Even though there won't be any plants growing on the back of this privacy wall, the frame looks just as good from the back as it does from the front, so rest assured it will be aesthetically pleasing to your neighbors too.

While this self-standing privacy wall was specifically designed to be used as a screen to add privacy to a deck, patio, or balcony, it could also be used to cover a boring blank wall or hide an unsightly area in the garden. Since it's not a permanent structure, you can easily move it to any area where you need a quick screen (to hide that ugly compost bin or rain barrel during a garden party, for example). Just be sure you always place the self-standing privacy wall on a flat, level surface before hanging the planters on it.

The frame for this vertical garden was made to hold hanging deck planter boxes that can be hooked over the top of a deck or balcony railing. The planter boxes I used are 20" wide, but deck or window planter boxes up to 30" wide will work as well.

As an added bonus, the frame was also designed to allow for easy installation of a drip irrigation system. Simply run the irrigation hose up the inside corner behind one of the legs and attach it flush against the wood using tubing clamps. Then run the dripper lines directly behind each of the crossbars that hold the baskets, and discreetly run the drippers into the planters. Setting your drip system on a timer will make it a snap to keep your planters perfectly watered, and nobody will ever know it's there. Boom—a self-standing AND self-watering privacy wall garden.

MATERIALS:	TOOLS:
2 × 4 × 8' boards (2)	Drill
2 × 6 × 8' board (1)	Table saw
2 × 2 × 8' boards (2)	Miter saw
1 × 2 × 8' boards (3)	Eye and ear protection
#8 × 1¼" screws (16)	Work gloves
#8 × 2" screws (16)	Tape measure
#8 × 3" screws (12)	Pencil
Hanging deck or window box planters (4)	Wood clamps
Wood glue	Soil scoop or trowel
Soilless potting mix (see page 137)	

CUT LIST:			
PART	DIMENSIONS	PIECES	MATERIAL
Side	2 × 4 × 6'	2	2 × 4 × 8' board
Top	2 × 4 × 2'	2	2 × 4 × 8' board
Feet	2' length, angles are cut at 3½ × 7"	4	2 × 6 × 8' board
Side	2 × 2 × 6'	2	2 × 2 × 8' board
Top & Bottom	2 × 2 × 1'	4	2 × 2 × 8' board
Basket Holder/Support	1 × 2 × 28"	8	1 × 2 × 8' board

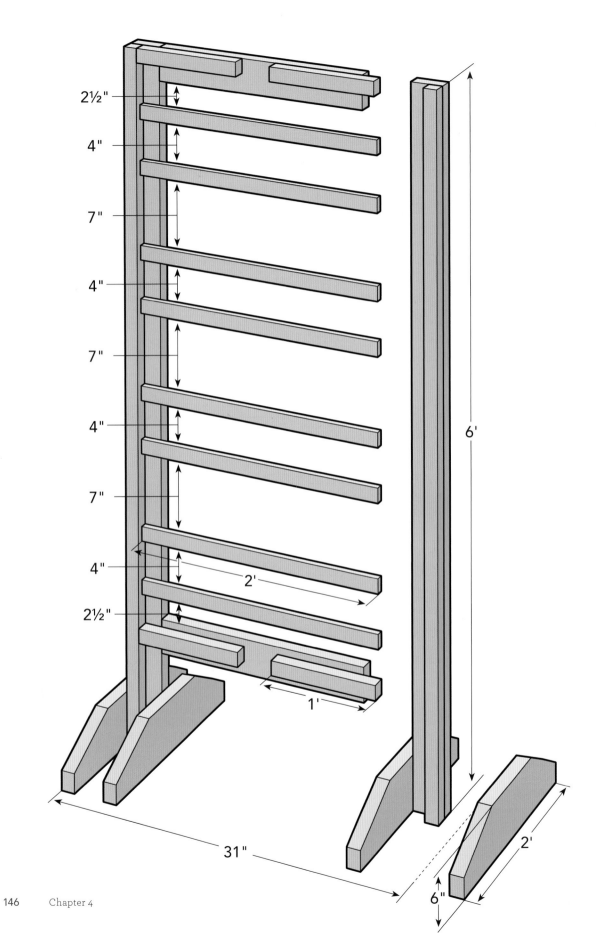

2½"

4"

7"

4"

7"

4"

7"

4"

2½"

2'

1'

6'

31"

6"

2'

How to Build a Self-Standing Privacy Wall Garden

STEP 1: Measure the length of each of the pieces and cut the lumber for the frame using a miter saw. Secure workpiece to miter gauge. Once all of the pieces are cut, cut 3½" × 7" angles on the top corner of each of the four feet.

STEP 2: Lay the four 2 × 4" pieces of wood for the frame down on a flat surface. Use wood glue to attach the four pieces, and then clamp the two sides together on the outside of the frame using clamps. Allow the glue to dry completely before moving on to the next step. Position both of the 2 × 2 × 6' boards so they sit parallel and are lined up with the outside of the frame. Predrill pilot holes and drive 2" screws through the 2 × 2 boards to attach each of them to the frame. To reinforce the corners of the frame, place one of the 2 × 2 × 1' boards at the top corner of the frame so that it's perpendicular with the 2 × 2 × 6' and sits flush with the top of the frame. Predrill pilot holes and drive 2" screws through the 2 × 2 board to attach it to the frame. Repeat with the remaining three 1' boards at each corner of the frame.

STEP 3: Measure 2½" down from the top of the frame and position the first 1 × 2 horizontal basket support so that it sits parallel to the top of the frame. Predrill pilot holes, then drive a 1¼" screw through each hole to attach the horizontal basket support piece to the frame. Measure 4" down from the first horizontal support to attach the next 1 × 2 board to the frame, and 7" down from the second to attach the third horizontal support to the frame. Repeat step to attach each of the remaining horizontal support pieces to the frame as shown in diagram. Depending on the size of the baskets you plan to hang, you may need to adjust your crossbar placement.

STEP 4: To attach the feet, lay the frame on one side, and position one of the 2 × 6 boards perpendicular to one of the legs of the frame. The angled corners of the foot should be facing up, and the bottom of the foot should sit even with the bottom of the frame leg. Predrill four pilot holes, then drive 3" screws through the foot and into the leg of the frame. Repeat step to attach the other three feet to the frame, one foot on the outside and one on the inside of each leg.

STEP 5: Once all four feet are attached to the frame, stand the frame up and place it on a level surface before hanging the baskets.

If you're not handy, or don't have time to build your own structures, you can find some very creative vertical container gardens for sale. This one kicks it up a notch by adding fantastic color to the patio garden.

5

PLANTERS *and* TOWERS

TAKE TRADITIONAL CONTAINER gardening to whole new heights by combining it with vertical gardening. When you mix these two methods together, you can come up with some fun and unusual ways to grow your own food. Plus, when you build your container garden up rather than out, you can grow exponentially more food in less space.

One of the biggest benefits of container gardening is that you can grow food in places you normally wouldn't be able to grow anything—for example, on your deck, balcony, or patio. Growing vegetables in containers and planters is also the perfect solution if you're dealing with poor-quality garden soil or a yard with limited space.

Plus, container gardening makes pest, disease, and weed control much easier, and helps to conserve water as well. Growing vegetables in containers makes fertilizing a cinch too, because you can give each plant the exact nutrients it needs to grow its best. Add in a simple drip irrigation system, and you have a self-watering vertical container garden that's basically no-maintenance!

The vertical gardening projects in this chapter are designed for growing anywhere, so you can make use of every bit of the prime sunny real estate that's available to you. An unused corner of your deck or balcony is the perfect spot to put a tower or stacked container garden. Build a tiered or trellised planter on your patio, or even on the driveway if that's the only sunny space that you have.

If you do have a yard but you can't grow plants in the ground because of poor quality or contaminated soil, thick tree roots, or rocky soil, then grow on top of it in a self-contained planter box with a built-in trellis!

This chapter is all about combining vertical gardening and container gardening. The projects you will find here include getting creative with containers and planters by building tower gardens, tiered or trellised planter boxes, and self-standing gardens.

CORNER TOWER GARDEN PLANTER

Tower gardens are a huge trend right now, and it's fun to get creative with the different styles and designs. This chapter features a few different versions of tower gardens, but this corner tower garden planter is the most complex. It was specifically created for the ambitious DIYer who's looking to get their hands on a more challenging project.

This unique tiered planter was designed to fit perfectly into an unused corner of a deck, patio, or garden, and it's ideal for adding height to commonly underutilized spaces. The top three tiers are bottomless, which makes the smaller containers deep enough for planting a variety of crops.

Add even more layers to your tiered planter by mixing plants of different heights, shapes, and sizes. Place the tallest plants, such as peppers and tomatoes, in the back, then add shorter crops, such as greens and herbs, in front. Be sure to include some trailing plants, such as strawberries or creeping herbs, to fill in the gaps and spill over the edges of the planter.

The basic idea behind this wood planting "tower" is a simple design that is easy to adapt and scale to your available space.

MATERIALS:	TOOLS:
Landscape timber, 8' (1)	Miter saw
1" × 6" × 10' deck boards (3)	Eye and ear protection
2 × 3 × 2' board (1)	Tape measure
2" finishing nails (80)	Pencil
2½" screws (16)	Work gloves
Container potting soil (see page 159)	Hammer or pneumatic nailer
	Drill
	Wood glue
	Soil scoop or trowel

CUT LIST:

PART	DIMENSIONS	PIECES	MATERIAL
Base	22"	6	Deck boards
1st tier (front)	27" at longest point*	2	Deck boards
1st tier (rear)	26" at longest point**	1	Deck boards
1st tier (rear)	24⅞" at longest point**	1	Deck boards
2nd tier (front)	21½" at longest point*	2	Deck boards
2nd tier (rear)	20¾" at longest point**	1	Deck boards
2nd tier (rear)	20½" at longest point**	1	Deck boards
3rd tier (front)	17" at longest point*	2	Deck boards
3rd tier (rear)	16½" at longest point**	1	Deck boards
3rd tier (rear)	14¾" at longest point**	1	Deck boards
4th tier (front)	10½" at longest point*	2	Deck boards
4th tier (rear)	8½" at longest point**	1	Deck boards
4th tier (rear)	9¾" at longest point**	1	Deck boards
Legs	4"	4	Landscape timber
2nd tier front support	4½"	1	Landscape timber
3rd tier front support	10½"	1	Landscape timber
4th tier front support	16½"	1	Landscape timber
Back corner support	21"	1	2 × 3 × 2'

* Front boards are cut on one end using the crown molding setting on a miter saw.

** Rear boards are cut on one end using a 38-degree angle on a miter saw.

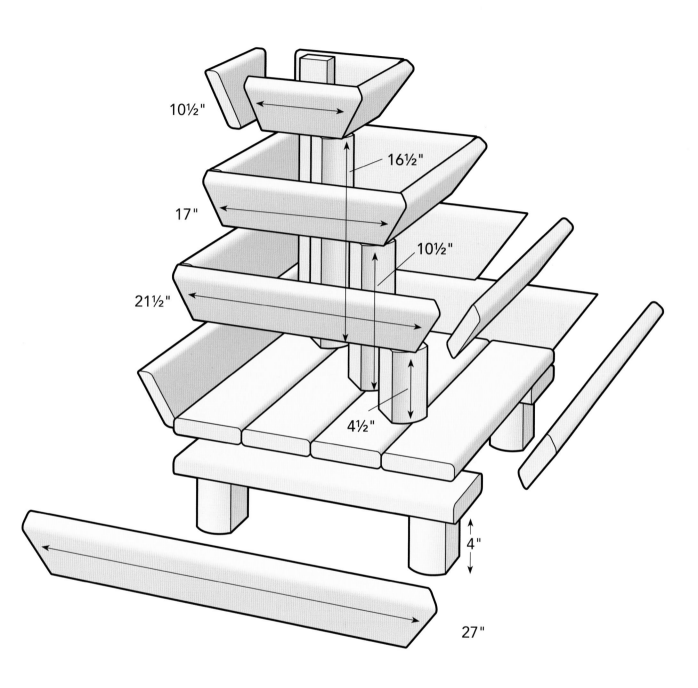

10½"

16½"

17"

10½"

21½"

4½"

4"

27"

How to Build a Corner Tower Garden Planter

STEP 1: Cut all of the boards to size, and then set the miter saw to the crown molding setting. Starting with the front board pieces, cut a crown molding angle into one end of each of the boards, leaving the other end of each board with a straight cut. Next, set the miter saw at a 38-degree angle, and cut an angle into one end of each of the rear board pieces, leaving the other end of each board with a straight cut. When complete, each of the boards for the sides of the tiered planter boxes will have one angled end and one straight end.

STEP 2: Lay two of the 22" deck board pieces on a flat surface so that they sit parallel to each other. Position the remaining four 22" boards so that they are perpendicular to and sitting on top of the two parallel boards. The ends of the boards on top should be flush and square with the edges of the bottom boards. Use nails or screws to attach the top boards to the bottom boards at each point where the boards cross.

STEP 3: Build the bottom tier planter box by first positioning the 26" rear board piece so that it sits parallel to one side of the base, and the bottom side of the board is flush with the bottoms of the four boards on the base. The bottom edge of the angled end should line up with one corner of the base, and the straight edge will overlap the other corner of the base. Attach the rear board to the base using nails. Position the 24⅞" piece so that the flat end is square against the flat side of the 26" rear board and the bottom edge of the board sits flush with the side of the base. Add glue to reinforce the corners, then use nails to secure the corners of the two boards together, and also to attach the bottom of the 24⅞" board to the base. Take one of the 27" boards and angle it so that the straight end of the board sits flush against the angled end of one of the rear boards. Add glue to secure the corners, ensure that they are square, and then use nails to secure the two boards together, and also to attach the bottom of the 27" board to the base. Install the other 27" board by angling it and fitting the crown molding cut ends of the two front boards together, add glue to both corners, and then attach the board to the base and the other two boards using nails. Assemble the planter boxes for the other three tiers using the same steps, only attaching the pieces to each other rather than attaching them to the base. At this point, you will have four individual planter tier boxes.

STEP 4: Stand all four of the legs up on a flat surface, and lay the base over the top so that each leg is centered under one corner of the base. Drill pilot holes through the base, then attach the base to the leg using three 3½" screws. Repeat this step to attach the other three legs to the base.

5

6

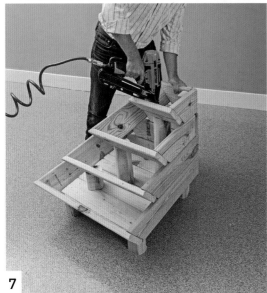

7

STEP 5: Stack the planter box for the second tier on top of the first tier so that the back is square with the back of the bottom tier. Place the 4½" timber support piece on top of the base, and position it so that it sits directly under the front corner of the second tier and the bottom corner of the angle sits flush with the front of the support piece. Use nails to attach the front corner of the planter box to the top of the support piece. At this point the back of the second tier will be sitting on top of the base and not attached yet.

STEP 6: Stack the third-tier planter box on top of the second so that the back corners are square. Stand the 10½" timber piece up on top of the base, and position it so that it sits directly under the front corner of the third tier, and so that the bottom angle of the planter is flush with the front of the timber support. Add a line of glue onto one side of the 21" 1 × 2 back support piece, and then place it vertically inside the planter so that it sits flush in the back corner and the bottom is sitting on top of the base. Ensure that all three tiers of the planter are square before drilling pilot holes, then attach all three tiers to the back support using the 2½" screws. Use nails to secure the front corner of the third-tier box to the top of the 10½" support piece.

STEP 7: Stack the fourth tier on top of the third tier and position the 16½" timber support under the front corner. Ensure the back of the top tier is square with the back of the planter box, and drill pilot holes before attaching it to the back support using 2½" screws. Attach the front corner of the fourth-tier planter box to the timber support using nails.

DIY Container Potting Soil Recipe

Unlike when you're growing in containers that hang from a wall, fence, or other structure, the weight of a planted container isn't important when you're growing vegetables in pots that sit on the ground. You can use a general purpose container potting soil like the one in this recipe.

Supplies needed:
Measuring container*
Shovel or trowel
Large container for mixing
Water (if the ingredients you're using are dry)

Container potting soil recipe:
2 parts peat moss, pre-moistened coconut coir,
   or basic potting soil
Garden lime**
2 parts compost or composted manure
1 part perlite
¼ to ½ part vermiculite

* I use a 1-gallon bucket, but you can use any size measuring container you want.
** Peat moss is acidic, and most vegetables and herbs prefer a more alkaline soil. So, if you use peat moss, you should add 1 tablespoon of garden lime per gallon of peat moss to your potting mix to balance out the acidity level. On the other hand, if you're growing plants that prefer an acidic soil (like berry plants), then don't add any garden lime to your mix.

Instructions:
Pour all of the ingredients into a large container, and use a shovel or trowel to stir them together until well mixed. Add water as you stir if your ingredients are extremely dry. Once everything is thoroughly mixed together, your potting soil can be used right away. Be sure to store any unused potting mix in a sealed container to keep bugs out.

PLANTER BOX WITH TRELLIS

Having a yard is wonderful, but sometimes gardeners are unable to grow plants directly in the ground. Maybe the soil is too rocky, or it's filled with tree roots. Or maybe you can't plant a garden directly in soil for a different reason . . .

A huge black walnut tree grows directly behind the fence that surrounds my parents' backyard. Sounds harmless to the unknowing, but black walnut trees are allelopathic plants, which means they excrete a natural chemical into the soil that is toxic to other plants. This toxin, called juglone, can kill or drastically stunt the growth of susceptible plants, including several types of vegetables, fruits, and herbs. Though beautiful, this troublesome tree has poisoned most of the soil in my parents' yard, making it impossible for them to grow a successful vegetable garden directly in the ground.

Raised planter boxes like the one in this project are the perfect solution for whatever ails your garden soil. One of the requirements for this design was that it had to have a closed bottom so the toxin that poisons my parents' ground wouldn't seep into the soil in the planter. Since it has a bottom, you can install this vertical gardening planter on top of concrete pavers if you also need to keep it from touching the soil (which is what we did), or it could be installed on top of a patio or deck.

The built-in trellis allows you to grow even more food in this small, self-contained garden, and, when strategically placed, it could double as a privacy screen. You could grow lightweight vines such as peas, cucamelons, or pole beans, but the trellis is large enough to support heavier crops such as cucumbers, mini melons, or indeterminate tomatoes as well. Just be sure to place your planter box in an area where it faces the sun, so the trellis won't end up shading the rest of the garden.

MATERIALS:	TOOLS:
1 × 6 × 12' deck boards (4)	Miter saw
1 × 2 × 8' boards (5)	Eye and ear protection
4 × 4 × 10' board (1)	Work gloves
4 × 4 × 6' board (1) (You'll only need 26½", so buy a shorter piece if you can.)	Tape measure
	Pencil
2 × 2 × 8' board (1)	Table saw
Carriage bolts ⅜" × 6", galvanized (2)	Drill
Washer galvanized for bolts (2)	⁹⁄₃₂" drill bit
2" screws (72)	½" socket wrench or drill adapter
1¼" nails (61)	Hammer or pneumatic nailer
Container potting soil (see page 159)	Wood glue
	Wood clamp
	Soil scoop or trowel

CUT LIST:			
PART	DIMENSIONS	PIECES	MATERIAL
Base (bottom of box)	36"	4	Deck boards
Base feet	22½"	3	Deck boards
Sides of box (short boards)	20"	4	Deck boards
Sides of box (long boards)	22½"	2	Deck boards
Front and back of box (short boards)	33¼"	2	Deck boards
Front and back of box (long boards)	36"	4	Deck boards
Inside vertical and horizontal supports	2 × 2 × 18"	6	2 × 2 board
Sides of trellis frame*	4 × 4 × 62½"	2	4 × 4 board
Top of trellis frame	4 × 4 × 26½"	1	4 × 4 board
Vertical support for lattice	1 × 2 × 41¾"	2	1 × 2 board
Horizontal support for lattice	1 × 2 × 26½"	2	1 × 2 board
Lattice pieces	1 × 2 × 12"	3	1 × 2 board
Lattice pieces	1 × 2 × 25"	4	1 × 2 board
Lattice pieces	1 × 2 × 37"	4	1 × 2 board
Lattice pieces	1 × 2 × 42"	1	1 × 2 board
Lattice pieces	1 × 2 × 36"	1	1 × 2 board
Lattice pieces	1 × 2 × 15"	1	1 × 2 board

* Simply cut a 4 × 4 × 10' board in half; the exact measurement of these two pieces may be slightly different, depending on where you buy your 10' board.

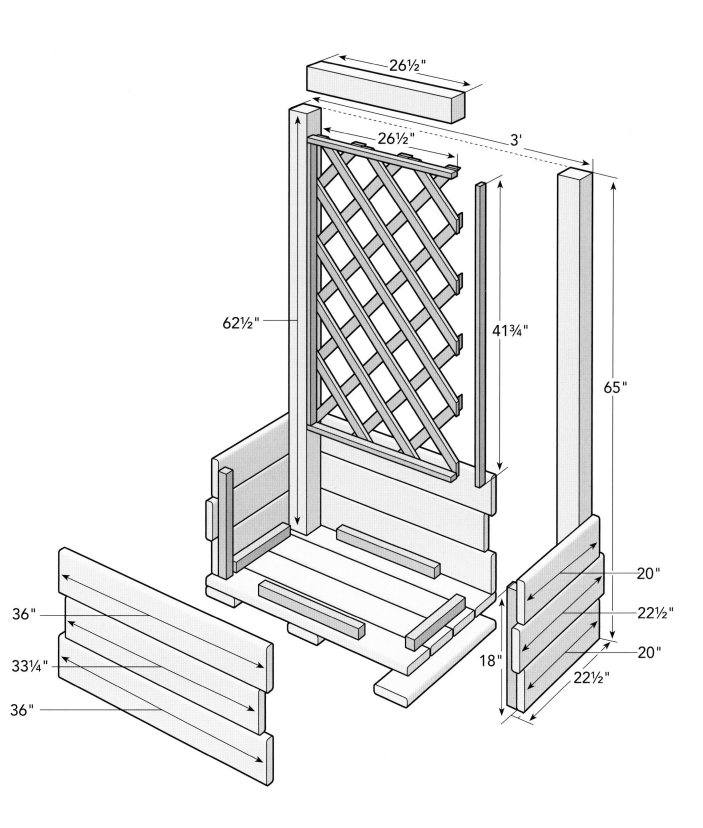

26½"

26½"

3'

62½"

41¾"

65"

36"

33¼"

36"

20"

22½"

20"

18"

22½"

How to Build a Planter Box With Trellis

1

2

3

STEP 1: Cut all of the boards to size, then lay four of the 36" boards on a flat surface so that they sit parallel to each other. Lay three of the 22½" boards perpendicularly over the four boards, positioning one so it's centered in the middle and the other two so they sit flush and square with the edges of the 36" boards. Drill pilot holes, and then use 2" screws to attach the top boards onto the bottom boards at each point where the boards cross each other. Flip the base over before moving on to the next step.

STEP 2: Starting with two 36" (outside) boards and two 20" (inside) boards, stack the deck boards on top of the base so that they are flush with all four corners on the inside of the base. Make sure the boards are square before predrilling pilot holes and attaching them together using 2" screws. Repeat this step using the two 33¼" boards and the two 22½" boards, staggering them so that the 33¼" board is on the outside of the 22½" board. Repeat the step again using the remaining 36" and 20" boards. At this point the three boxes won't be attached to the base or to each other yet; they are just stacked on top of each other.

STEP 3: Starting with one of the 2 × 2 × 18" inside support pieces, run a line of wood glue over one side of the brace support, and then place it in the bottom corner on one side of the box. Predrill pilot holes, and then use screws to attach the side of the box to the horizontal support, and also to attach the support to the base. Repeat with the remaining three 2 × 2 × 18" support pieces, placing one support in the bottom corner of each of the three remaining sides of the box, and then attaching them to both the side and bottom of the box. The two remaining 2 × 2 × 18" boards are vertical supports for the front corners of the box, and will be used to attach the three layers of the box together. Run a line of glue along one side of one of the support pieces, and place it vertically in the front corner on one side of the box. Predrill pilot holes, and then drive screws through the support piece into each layer of the box to secure the layers together. Repeat with the second vertical brace support in the other front corner.

STEP 4: Lay two of the 4 × 4 × 62½" pieces of wood on a flat surface so they are parallel to each other, then lay the 4 × 4 × 26½" board perpendicularly between the tops of the two 62½" boards. Ensure the top of the 26½" board sits flush with the top of the 62½" boards, and that the boards are square. Apply glue and clamp the parts together with a wood clamp.

STEP 5: Use a ⁹⁄₃₂" drill bit to drill a hole all the way through each of the 62½" boards into the 26½" board for the carriage bolts. Remove the clamp and then use an impact driver with a nut driver or use a ratcheting socket wrench to tighten both of the bolts.

STEP 6: Place the trellis frame into the box so that the bottoms of the 62½" boards are sitting on the base and are flush with the back corners of the box. Predrill pilot holes, and then drive 2" screws through the back and the sides of each of the planter boards to attach the trellis frame to the box.

7

STEP 7: Place one of the 1 × 2 × 26½″ horizontal lattice support pieces flat against the top of the trellis frame so that it sits flush with the front of the frame, and attach it using finishing nails. Starting on one side of the trellis frame, position one of the 1 × 2 × 41¾″ vertical lattice support pieces so that it sits flush with the front of the trellis frame and is square with the top lattice support piece, then attach it using finishing nails. Repeat this step to install the two remaining vertical and horizontal support pieces, resulting in a rectangle around the inside of the trellis frame.

Starting in the top left corner on the back of the frame, position one 12″ lattice piece so that it sits flush in the corner on the outside of the lattice support and at a 45-degree angle to the frame. Mark lines on each end of the lattice piece for the angles, and then use the miter saw to cut the angles. Line the lattice piece up again and attach the ends to the top and side lattice support pieces using finishing nails. Repeat to install a 25″ lattice piece, then two 37″ pieces, one 36″, one 25″, and one 15″ piece 4½″ apart, attaching each end of each piece to the lattice support frame. Then, starting at the top right corner, install one 12″ lattice piece so that it runs perpendicular to the installed lattice pieces, then use finishing nails to attach it at each point where it crosses the other lattice pieces. Repeat to install the 25″, 37″, 42″, 37″, 25″, and 12″ pieces respectively.

Vegetables That Will Tolerate the Juglone Toxin

Don't worry; having a black walnut tree in your yard isn't all gloom and doom for the gardener. It's frustrating, but just because you have a black walnut tree doesn't mean you can't grow vegetables.

Rest assured, there are plants that are tolerant of the juglone toxin, including some vegetables and other edible crops. Do a quick internet search, and you'll find a wealth of information about gardening with black walnut trees, including lists of many types of garden plants that are immune to the toxin.

To get you started, here's a list of vegetables that are tolerant of the juglone toxin:

Vining crops: squash, melons, cucumbers, beans

Root crops: beets, onions, garlic, parsnips, carrots

Herbs: parsley

Other vegetables: corn, cauliflower, leeks

STACKED POTS TOWER GARDEN

If you're like me, you have more planters collecting dust in the garage than you care to admit. What better way to put those extra planters to use than to create a stacked pot tower garden? Not only does it look great; a tower garden keeps your crops out of reach of pesky critters looking for a snack.

Don't worry; your containers don't have to be exactly the same. Have fun with it by mixing different shapes, patterns, or colors to make it really unique. The most important thing to remember when choosing your pots is that all three of them need to have drainage holes. Many decorative containers come with a plug in the bottom that can simply be removed to create adequate drainage. If the pots you plan to use don't have drainage holes, use a large drill bit to add them (use a masonry bit to drill holes in clay or ceramic pots).

It's also very important to build your stacked tower garden on a spot that is level so the tower won't topple. I used a decorative paver as a level base for mine, which makes it easy to put this tower garden anywhere.

MATERIALS:	TOOLS:
3 decorative containers (1 large, 1 medium, and 1 small)	Drill
2 cachepots (1 large and 1 small)	Large drill bit
Container potting soil (see page 159)	Small level
	Tape measure or ruler
	Soil scoop or trowel
	Eye protection
	Work gloves

How to Build a Stacked Pots Tower Garden

STEP 1: If your decorative pots have plugs in the bottoms, remove the plugs to allow for drainage. Otherwise, use a large drill bit to make holes in the bottoms of all three decorative pots (if they don't already have drainage holes).

STEP 2: Place the large cachepot upside down in the center of the largest decorative container. Add some potting soil to the bottom of the container if necessary to help position the cachepot so that the bottom will be level with the soil line once the decorative container is full. Use a tape measure to ensure that the cachepot is centered in the container.

STEP 3: Place the large decorative container in a spot that is completely level. Then use a level to ensure the cachepot sits level inside the decorative container so that the tower isn't lopsided.

STEP 4: Begin filling the decorative container with container potting soil, gently packing it down to secure the cachepot in place as you work. Stop when the container is about half full to check that the cachepot is still level and adjust it if it has shifted. Once the container is full enough, plant it by positioning plants all around the outside of the cachepot. Then fill the gaps around the plants so that the soil level in the decorative container is even with the bottom of the cachepot. Repeat steps 2 through 4 using the medium-sized decorative container and the small cachepot. Then simply fill the smallest container with soil and plant it.

STEP 5: Stack the pots by first placing the medium-sized container on top of the cachepot in the large container, and then placing the small container on top of the cachepot in the medium-sized container.

4

5

Note:
The upside-down cachepots are optional—you can just set the containers on top of the soil instead. But they do help to add stability, and they make it easier to level the stacked pots so that the tower won't be lopsided. They also work as a filler to help save money on potting soil.

STRAWBERRY TOWER GARDEN

One of the biggest advantages of growing food vertically is that it keeps your crops out of the reach of hungry critters. A vertical tower garden does just that, and it's a great way to grow strawberries.

An added benefit of growing strawberries in this tower garden is that it makes harvesting much easier. No more squatting down and searching around along the ground for strawberries. The strawberries hang down all around the tower, making it easy to spot all the bright berries that are ripe for picking.

This simple project is a great way to use up leftover materials you probably have sitting in your garage. Because of the amount of soil that is required to fill the tower, a piece of drain tile tubing was added into the center of the tower to make watering easier and to ensure all of the plants get evenly watered.

MATERIALS:	TOOLS:
Large decorative container (I used a 14" pot)	Wire cutters
Large cachepot that fits into the decorative container (I used a 12" pot)	Fabric shears
	Drill
16-gauge, 3'-tall metal garden fencing (mine was cut to 46" long)	Drill bit
Landscaping fabric (mine was cut to 58" long)	PVC saw
Corrugated drain tile pipe (also called drainage tile or drain tile)	Clothespins (or similar clips)
Drain tile pipe endcap	Work gloves
Wire ties (optional)	Soil scoop or trowel
Container potting soil (see page 159)	Eye protection
	Tape measure

Note: If your decorative pot doesn't already have drainage holes in the bottom, be sure to drill holes in it before starting this project.

What Is Corrugated Drain Tile?

Corrugated drain tile is a misleading name, because it's not tile at all. Corrugated drain tile (a.k.a. drainage tile) is simply a piece of plastic tubing that has holes or slits in it. Drainage tile is commonly used in landscaping as a way to add drainage to an area where water tends to pool. It's also commonly used in construction to keep water away from basements and building foundations. Drainage tile can be found in the gardening or plumbing section of any home improvement store. Drainage tile is convenient for this project because it already has holes cut in the plastic. But you could use any type of plastic tubing you may have on hand. Simply drill holes along the entire length of the tubing.

How to Build a Strawberry Tower Garden

STEP 1: Determine how long your wire fencing needs to be by wrapping it around the cachepot. Use wire cutters to cut the fencing, leaving the wires long enough so that you can use them as tabs to secure the fencing together. Measure and cut your landscaping fabric so that it's 12" longer than the fencing.

STEP 2: Form a cylinder out of the fencing by wrapping it around the outside of the cachepot, and attach the ends together using the overlapping tabs of fencing. Be sure to secure the fencing down the entire length of the seam so it won't pop open. Use wire ties if necessary to secure the fencing together.

STEP 3: Place the cylinder and cachepot into the decorative container, gently pushing it all the way down into the decorative container. The fencing should be snug between the cachepot and the decorative pot. Roll up the landscaping fabric the long way, and place it in the center of the cylinder. Unroll the landscaping fabric around the inside of the cylinder, straightening it and securing it to the fencing with clothespins to hold it in place as you work.

STEP 4: To determine the length of the corrugated drain tile, measure from the top of the cachepot to the top of the cylinder fencing. Use the PVC saw to cut the drainage tile to the correct length. Drill drainage holes in the drain tile pipe end cap, and then place it on one end of the drainage tile.

STEP 5: Start by filling only the cachepot with soil. Next, place the drainage tile tubing inside the center of the cylinder so the end cap sits on top of the soil. Ensure the top of the tubing is even with the top of the fencing. Hold the tubing in place in the center of the cylinder, and slowly fill the cylinder with soil (try not to get any soil in the drain tile tube as you fill the tower). Straighten and tighten the landscaping fabric as you fill the cylinder with soil.

STEP 6: Once the cylinder is filled with soil, remove the clothespins and cut off any excess landscaping fabric around the top of the cylinder.

STEP 7: To plant your tower garden, cut a slit in the landscaping fabric where the plant will go. Loosen the soil with your fingers, and gently press the roots of the plant into the soil.

Tip:
Save a little money on soil by filling the bottom of your cachepot with empty plastic bottles (or other lightweight material) before filling the tower with soil. The bottles will take up space, saving on soil and also making your tower garden a little lighter.

Dirt Is Dirt, Right?

When it comes to growing your own food, any seasoned gardener will tell you that the soil makes all the difference in the world. "Dirt is dirt" is a common misconception of new gardeners and one of the main reasons why they struggle to grow an abundance of their own food.

Another common mistake new gardeners make is filling their containers with garden soil. The plants grow great in your garden, so why wouldn't that same soil work in containers too? Unfortunately, this is a recipe for disaster.

Garden soil, topsoil, and other types of cheap dirt are too heavy for use in containers and will quickly become compacted, making it extremely difficult for the plants to flourish.

Soil is the foundation in which plants grow, so it's essential to always start with high-quality soil. This is especially true for growing vegetables in containers, since they rely on us to provide all of the nutrients they need to survive and produce healthy food.

For growing vegetables in containers, you want a fluffy, porous potting mix that allows water and air to reach the roots of the plants and won't become compacted in the container. Container potting soil should have good drainage but also hold moisture, and it should be rich in the nutrients that vegetables need to thrive.

You can find high-quality potting soil that is specifically made for container gardening at any garden center or home improvement store, or you can mix your own using the recipe on page 159.

SELF-STANDING GUTTER GARDEN

Gutter gardens are super-popular these days, and I absolutely adore the idea. But all of the designs I have seen require a sturdy spot to hang them. The gutters become very heavy once they're filled with plants and soil, especially after watering them, and I don't have a spot that's sturdy enough to safely hold all of that weight. So I decided to come up with a fun design for a self-standing gutter garden that doesn't require hanging.

This design uses metal gutters and pipes that can be found at any home improvement store. I used precut, threaded metal pipes to make the project much easier. No pipe cutter required! If you don't like the idea of using metal for this project, you could easily adapt it to use materials made out of PVC.

This self-standing gutter garden is perfect for any area in your yard and offers an impressive amount of growing space. My gutter garden was planted with a mix of salad greens and herbs, but strawberries would grow just as well in these shallow planters.

MATERIALS:	TOOLS:
10' metal gutter (1)	Hacksaw
Left gutter endcaps (4)	Tin snips
Right gutter endcaps (4)	Screwdriver
48" threaded ½" black steel pipes (2)	Level
36" threaded ½" black steel pipe (1)	Hammer (optional—to pound pipes into the ground
30" threaded ½" black steel pipes (2)	if necessary)
½" black metal pipe caps (5)	Work gloves
Size 8 stainless steel pipe clamps (11)	Eye protection
Polyurethane glue	Ear protection (optional—needed if pounding pipes
Spray paint (optional—I used hammered copper)	into the ground)
Soilless potting mix (see page 137)	Soil scoop or trowel

CUT LIST:			
PART	DIMENSIONS	PIECES	MATERIAL
Gutter planters	2½'	4	Gutter

Note: The edges of the metal gutters are extremely sharp, so be sure to wear work gloves at all times when handling or cutting the gutter pieces.

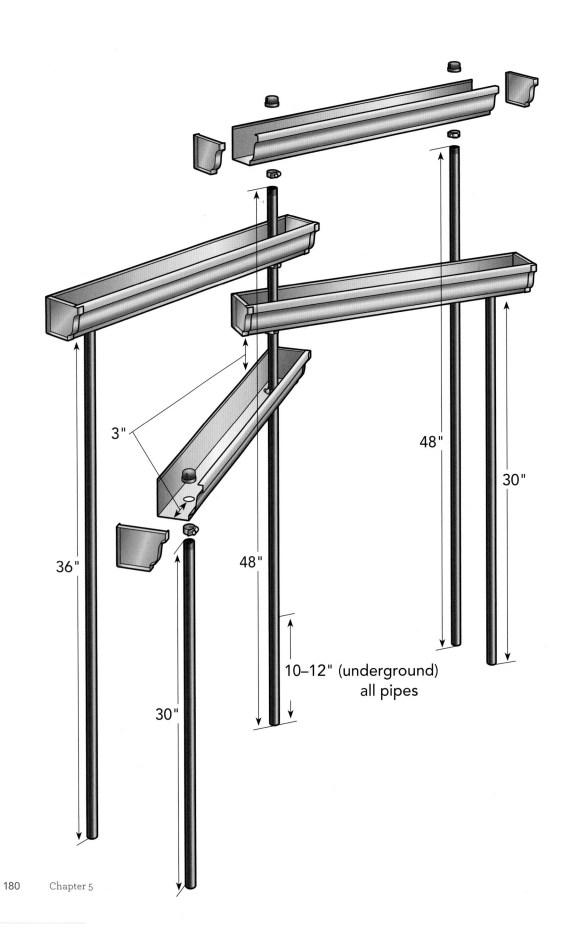

3"

48"

30"

36"

48"

10–12" (underground)
all pipes

30"

How to Build a Self-Standing Gutter Garden

STEP 1: Use the hacksaw to cut the gutter pieces to size. The cuts don't have to be perfectly straight, since they will be covered by the endcaps, but cut them as straight as you can.

STEP 2: Measure 3" from each end of each of the gutter pieces, and mark the spots where the holes will go. The holes should be slightly closer to the fronts of the gutters than the backs. Use tin snips to cut holes that are just large enough for the pipes to fit through (the pipes should fit snugly into the holes). Take care not to make the holes too large, or the pipe clamps may not hold the gutters tightly.

STEP 3: Fit the gutter endcaps over each end of the gutter pieces, and then glue them on, pressing firmly on the endcaps to ensure a good fit. Allow the glue to dry completely before moving on to the next step.

> **Note:**
> If you choose to spray paint the gutters like I did, you can paint them at any time. But you might find it easier to pause here and paint them before moving to the next steps for assembling the gutter garden.

STEP 4: Drive the center pipe into the ground first, and then measure the space between the holes in each of the gutter pieces to determine how far apart to space the pipes. Drive each of the pipes into the ground deep enough so it is are stable. Use a hammer to pound them in if the ground is too hard to push the pipes in manually.

STEP 5: Slide one pipe clamp onto each of the pipes before adding the gutters. Starting with the bottom gutter, slide the gutter onto the middle pipe and then onto the top of the shortest pipe.

STEP 6: Screw one of the pipe caps onto the top of the shortest pipe over the gutter, then press the gutter firmly into the bottom of the pipe cap.

Tip:
Soaking the ground with water the night before will help to soften it and make it easier to push the pipes in.

STEP 7: Slide the pipe clamp on the shortest pipe up to the bottom of the gutter, sandwiching the gutter securely between the pipe cap and the pipe clamp. Use a screwdriver to tighten the pipe clamp, securing the gutter in place. Ensure the other side of the gutter is level on the center pipe, and then slide the pipe clamp on the center pipe up to the bottom of the gutter. Use a screwdriver to tighten the pipe clamp and hold the gutter in place. Slide another pipe clamp onto the center pipe and press it down over the top of the gutter, sandwiching the gutter between the two pipe clamps to hold it firmly in place. Use a screwdriver to tighten the pipe clamp. Repeat steps 5 through 7 to install the remaining three gutters, sliding a pipe clamp onto the center pipe each time before adding the next gutter piece.

7

UPCYCLED UTILITY RACK PLANTER

Some of the best places to get inspiration for DIY projects are discount stores and thrift shops. This project gives new life to a simple utility rack that I found at a local discount store, turning it into a vertical garden planter. A beverage cart or other decorative storage cart would also work great. Just make sure it's made out of a durable material that can stand up to the elements outdoors.

My upcycled utility rack planter came on wheels, which is a bonus for me. The wheels make it easy to move my vertical garden planter around on the deck, and I can simply roll it into the porch when there's a threat of frost. If yours doesn't have wheels, you could easily add some inexpensive wheels, which can be found at any home improvement store.

For this project, I chose to line the wire baskets of my utility rack with coco liners because I like how they look with the color of the rack that I bought. But you could use landscaping fabric or burlap to line the baskets if you prefer. Coco liners can be found at any garden center or home improvement store, and they come in either preformed sizes or in large rolls.

MATERIALS:	TOOLS:
Metal wire basket utility rack or beverage cart	Scissors
Coco liners	Work gloves
3" cable zip ties	Soil scoop or trowel
Container potting soil (see page 159)	

Note: If your utility rack is made out of a different material (such as wood or solid metal), make sure to drill a few drainage holes in the bottom of each planter so water doesn't pool in the bottom.

How to Create an Upcycled Utility Rack Planter

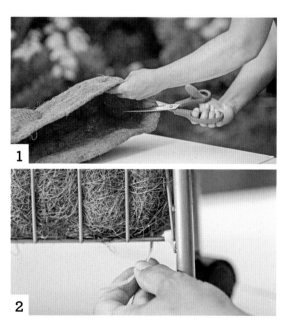

STEP 1: Measure the inside dimensions of each of the baskets to determine the size of your coco liner pieces, then use scissors to cut the liners to size.

STEP 2: Starting with one basket, center the coco liner inside the basket, and then press the liner into the corners of the basket. Secure one corner of the liner, using a zip tie to hold it in place. Work your way around the inside of the basket, straightening the liner as you go and using zip ties to secure it to the wire basket every few inches. Repeat steps 1 and 2 to add the coco liner to the remaining baskets.

METRIC CONVERSIONS

Metric Equivalent

	1/64	1/32	1/25	1/16	1/8	1/4	3/8	2/5	1/2	5/8	3/4	7/8	1	2	3	4	5	6	7	8	9	10	11	12	36	39.4
Inches (in.)	1/64	1/32	1/25	1/16	1/8	1/4	3/8	2/5	1/2	5/8	3/4	7/8	1	2	3	4	5	6	7	8	9	10	11	12	36	39.4
Feet (ft.)																								1	3	3 1/12
Yards (yd.)																									1	1 1/12
Millimeters (mm)	0.40	0.79	1	1.59	3.18	6.35	9.53	10	12.7	15.9	19.1	22.2	25.4	50.8	76.2	101.6	127	152	178	203	229	254	279	305	914	1,000
Centimeters (cm)							0.95	1	1.27	1.59	1.91	2.22	2.54	5.08	7.62	10.16	12.7	15.2	17.8	20.3	22.9	25.4	27.9	30.5	91.4	100
Meters (m)																								.30	.91	1.00

Converting Measurements

TO CONVERT:	TO:	MULTIPLY BY:	TO CONVERT:	TO:	MULTIPLY BY:
Inches	Millimeters	25.4	Millimeters	Inches	0.039
Inches	Centimeters	2.54	Centimeters	Inches	0.394
Feet	Meters	0.305	Meters	Feet	3.28
Yards	Meters	0.914	Meters	Yards	1.09
Miles	Kilometers	1.609	Kilometers	Miles	0.621
Square inches	Square centimeters	6.45	Square centimeters	Square inches	0.155
Square feet	Square meters	0.093	Square meters	Square feet	10.8
Square yards	Square meters	0.836	Square meters	Square yards	1.2
Cubic inches	Cubic centimeters	16.4	Cubic centimeters	Cubic inches	0.061
Cubic feet	Cubic meters	0.0283	Cubic meters	Cubic feet	35.3
Cubic yards	Cubic meters	0.765	Cubic meters	Cubic yards	1.31
Pints (U.S.)	Liters	0.473 (Imp. 0.568)	Liters	Pints (U.S.)	2.114 (Imp. 1.76)
Quarts (U.S.)	Liters	0.946 (Imp. 1.136)	Liters	Quarts (U.S.)	1.057 (Imp. 0.88)
Gallons (U.S.)	Liters	3.785 (Imp. 4.546)	Liters	Gallons (U.S.)	0.264 (Imp. 0.22)
Ounces	Grams	28.4	Grams	Ounces	0.035
Pounds	Kilograms	0.454	Kilograms	Pounds	2.2
Tons	Metric tons	0.907	Metric tons	Tons	1.1

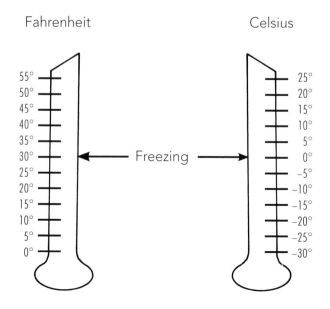

Fahrenheit / Celsius — Freezing

Converting Temperatures

Convert degrees Fahrenheit (F) to degrees Celsius (C) by following this simple formula: Subtract 32 from the Fahrenheit temperature reading. Then mulitply that number by $5/9$. For example, 77°F - 32 = 45. 45 × $5/9$ = 25°C.

To convert degrees Celsius to degrees Fahrenheit, multiply the Celsius temperature reading by $9/5$, then add 32. For example, 25°C × $9/5$ = 45. 45 + 32 = 77°F.

INDEX

PHOTOGRAPHY CREDITS

Photography by Tracy Walsh, except the following:

AMY ANDRYCHOWICZ: pages 6–7, 8–9, 15, 16, 18 left, 19, 20 top, 21 right, 22 left, 23 bottom left, 23 bottom right, 24 top left, 25, 26, 27, 28 right, 31 left, 34, 37, 38, 43, 44, 45, 46, 47, 48, 50, 51, 55, 56, 58, 59, 60, 61, 63, 64, 83, 137, 159, 167

JESSICA WALLISER: pages 5, 14, 18 right, 20 bottom left, 20 bottom right, 22 right, 24 top right, 24 bottom, 28 left, 31 right, 35, 39, 41, 42, 62

NIKI JABBOUR: pages 23 top, 36, 40

ERIC KRAUS: pages 13 top, 54 bottom

TARA NOLAN: page 150

SHUTTERSTOCK: page 13 bottom, rootstock; 32, Laszlo Szelenczey; 49, Marsan; 110 komkrit Preechachanwate

ABOUT THE AUTHOR

AMY ANDRYCHOWICZ is the creator of Get Busy Gardening, a popular gardening website dedicated to beginner gardeners, where she has been actively blogging for almost ten years. She is also the author of several successful eBooks that are available on GetBusyGardening.com.

After purchasing her first home in 2002, Amy discovered that she has a knack for designing and building DIY projects. Over the years, she has transformed her boring suburban yard into a garden oasis by adding several flower gardens, a large vegetable garden, a tropical garden, a rain garden, a Zen garden, two ponds, and many unique hardscape features—all of which were DIY projects.

Amy got her green thumb from her parents and has been gardening for most of her life. She is a passionate gardener who enjoys growing vegetables, herbs, annuals, perennials, succulents, tropical plants, and houseplants—you name, she's grown it! She is devoted to helping new gardeners learn through guidance, encouragement, and advice that is easy to understand. Amy loves sharing her knowledge, and strongly believes that there is no such thing as a brown thumb; anyone can be a gardener if they want to be.

When she's not gardening, you'll find Amy and her husband traveling, enjoying outdoor activities, and spending time with friends and family. Amy lives and gardens in Minneapolis, Minnesota (zone 4b), with her husband and two cats—though the cats aren't much help in the garden!

Follow Amy online:
Website: getbusygardening.com
Facebook: facebook.com/GetBusyGardening
Pinterest: pinterest.com/aschune
Instagram: @getbusygardening
Twitter: @getbusygardenin (yes, without the G at the end)